The Staff of Oedipus 🙰

Corporealities: Discourses of Disability

The Staff of Oedipus ⌒

Transforming DISABILITY
in
ANCIENT GREECE

Martha L. Rose

THE UNIVERSITY OF MICHIGAN PRESS ⌒ ANN ARBOR

FOR
Society for Disability Studies members ∾

First paperback edition 2013
Copyright © by the University of Michigan 2003
All rights reserved
Published in the United States of America by
The University of Michigan Press
Printed and bound by CPI Group (UK) Ltd, Croydon, CR0 4YY

2016 2015 2014 2013   5 4 3 2

A CIP catalog record for this book is available from the British Library.

Library of Congress Cataloging-in-Publication Data

Rose, Martha L., 1957–
    The staff of Oedipus : transforming disability in ancient Greece /
Martha L. Rose.
        p. cm. — (Corporealities)
    Includes bibliographical references and index.
    ISBN 978-0-472-11339-2 (Cloth : alk. paper)
    1. People with disabilities—Greece.   I. Title.   II. Series.
HV3024.G8 R67   2003
362.4'0938—dc21   2003002120

ISBN 978-0-472-03573-1 (paper : alk. paper)
ISBN 978-0-472-02626-5 (e-book)

Cover illustration: *Oedipus and Antigone at Colonus,* Johann Peter
Krafft, courtesy The Minneapolis Institute of Arts.

Poems with Disabilities ❧

I'm sorry—this space is reserved
for poems with disabilities. I know
it's one of the best spaces in the book,
but the Poems with Disabilities Act
requires us to make reasonable
accommodations for poems that aren't
normal. There is a nice space just
a few pages over—in fact (don't
tell anyone) I think it's better
than this one. I myself prefer it.
Actually I don't see any of those
poems right now myself, but you never know
when one might show up, so we have to keep
this space open. You can't always tell
just from looking at them, either. Sometimes
they'll look just like a regular poem
when they roll in—you're reading along
and suddenly everything
changes, the world tilts
a little, angle of vision
jumps, focus
shifts. You remember
your aunt died of cancer at just your age
and maybe yesterday's twinge means
something after all. Your sloppy,
fragile heart beats
a little faster
and then you know.
You just know.
And the poem is right
where it
belongs.

—Jim Ferris

Preface ∾

Scholars are sometimes puzzled to see the marriage of ancient history and disability studies, but the union is both suitable and fruitful. As the epigraph for this book expresses, disability is a universal human experience. Disability is an aspect of social history, like gender and age, and the phenomenon of disability intersects with and sheds light on economic, political, military, and religious aspects of any given society.

The ancient world has enchanted me since my early childhood, and throughout my education I maintained a passion for the ancient world and acquired another for disability studies. Through my friendships with disabled people, I became interested in disability issues and disability rights when I was doing my undergraduate work in history at the University of Minnesota in Minneapolis. When it came time to choose a topic for my Ph.D. dissertation—which I also completed at the University of Minnesota—disability in the ancient Greek world seemed a natural choice.

This book began as my dissertation project, and I am grateful to the many people who helped me through that process. Roberta Cullen, Lorna Sopçak, and Ross Willits, the members of my writing group in Minneapolis, were involved in the project from its very beginnings. Many generous scholars went out of their way to help me. I thank Lawrence Bliquez, Lois Bragg, Alan Boegehold, Lennard Davis, Robert Garland, Stephanos Geroulanos, Harlan Hahn, Anthony Hogan, and Nicholas Vlahogiannis. My dissertation committee members at the University of Minnesota—John Evans, Thomas Kelly, Nita Krevans, Philip Sellew, and Romeyn Taylor—gave their time as if they had it to spare. Above all, Thomas Kelly never allowed the smallest corner to be cut during the decade he served as my advisor, and I am grateful for his painstaking guidance.

As the dissertation became a book, my debt to my colleagues increased. Douglas Baynton, Lois Bragg, Jean Campbell, David Gerber, Miriam Hertz, Catherine Kudlick, Simi Linton, Paul Longmore, David Mitchell, James Trent, and D. P. M. Weerakkody have all contributed in one way or another to my scholarship.

I sincerely thank the members of the Down Under Writing Group—Natalie Alexander, David Christiansen, Janet Davis, Rebecca Harrison, William Hutton, and Bridget Thomas—who read countless versions of the manuscript. Three anonymous readers from the University of Michigan Press, along with the press's senior editor, LeAnn Fields, also offered excellent suggestions.

I am grateful for several Truman State University Faculty Research grants and for the assistance of Melissa Clark, Monika Kump, and Heather Tylock, all Truman State University students at one time. I am especially grateful for the assistance of Anna Hirsch.

The book includes some pieces of poetry, and I am very grateful to the poets for allowing me to use their work here. I thank Jim Ferris for permission to use "Poems with Disabilities," Lynn Manning for permission to use "The Magic Wand," and Cheryl Marie Wade for permission to use an excerpt of "I Am Not One Of The." Also included are several illustrations. I thank the staff of Art Resource for their help with figures 1 and 3 and their permission to reproduce them; Nikolaos Kaltsas, director of the National Archaeological Museum in Athens, for his permission to include figure 2; Jane Fraser, president of the Stuttering Foundation of America, for permission to include the foundation's public service advertisement; and the Minneapolis Institute of Arts for permission to reproduce figure 5. Portions of essays published elsewhere are integrated into this book. Many of the main ideas of chapter 2 were originally published in essays in the *Ancient History Bulletin* and *Ancient World*. I thank Taylor & Francis for permission to use "Deaf and Dumb in Ancient Greece" as the basis for chapter 4. This was first published in *The Disability Studies Reader*, copyright 1997, edited by Lennard Davis. Reproduced by permission of Routledge, Inc., part of The Taylor & Francis Group.

Barry Edwards supported me in large and small ways, with unwavering patience and grace. I received ongoing encouragement and both intellectual stimulation and grounding when I needed it most from David and Jean Adams, Marc Becker, Janet Davis, Julia DeLancey, William Edwards, Karen Hagrup, Wendy Hellerstedt, Anna Hirsch, Jerrold Hirsch, Paul Mueller, Cheryl Musch, Sherri Palmer, David Robinson, Frank Rose, Domino Rose, Mary Kay Speggen, Sue and Torbjörn Wandel, Sally West, and Thomas Zoumaras. I especially thank my husband, Steven Reschly, for all of his help.

Everyone mentioned here should be credited with any high points in this book. I alone am responsible for inaccuracies, infelicities, and mistakes.

Contents ∾

Abbreviations ∾

ACIT   Ludwig Edelstein and Emma Edelstein, *Asclepius: A Collection and Interpretation of the Testimonies*

FGrH   Felix Jacoby, *Die Fragmente der Griechischen Historiker*

PCG   R. Kassel and C. Austin, *Poetae Comici Graeci*

PMG   D. L. Page, *Poetae Melici Graeci*

P. Mich.   *The Michigan Papyri*

P. Oxy.   *The Oxyrhynchus Papyri*

P. Tebt.   *The Tebtunis Papyri*

SEG   *Supplementum Epigraphicum Graecum*

Sel. Pap.   *Selected Papyri* (Loeb Classical Library)

Introduction ∾

A newspaper article from January 2001 outlines the ethical debates around saving the lives of high-risk infants who, if they survive, are at risk for later disability.[1] Diana Aitchison concludes that decisions over whether or not to let a baby die rest on a gamble: "Which babies will, even with disabilities, grow to make major contributions to society, like Helen Keller, Stevie Wonder or physicist Stephen Hawking, and which will rely on public medical assistance all their lives is anybody's guess."[2] This article highlights issues that must be part of any investigation in the history of disability: economic assumptions about disability, the idea that a disabled person must make extraordinary contributions to society in order to be worthy, and the categorization of people according to their medical status.

Physical disability considered as a social construct rather than as a medical condition constitutes a valuable category of analysis for ancient social history. Karen Hagrup explains that "the introduction of a disabled/nondisabled dimension in historical studies brings to light new issues not revealed by familiar categories such as gender, class, race, ethnicity, age, occupation, or rural versus urban settings."[3] I examine ancient Greek material through the lens of disability studies, which approaches the phenomenon of disability by assuming that there is nothing inherently wrong with the disabled body and that the reaction of a society to the disabled body is neither predictable nor immutable.

Looking at disability in the ancient world from the perspective of disability studies has led me to make two major, interrelated points throughout this book. First, our assumptions about the place of people with disabilities in the present day have colored, often falsely, our interpretations about people with disabilities in the ancient world. Second, these skewed interpretations of the ancient world bolster modern discriminatory attitudes toward people with disability, giving the attitudes an apparent historical precedent.

The Greek material that mentions or depicts physical disability comes from a wide variety of sources, and mention is rarely overt. One of the contributing factors to this state of the evidence is that the Greeks did not perceive a category of physical disability in which people were a priori banned from carrying out certain roles and compartmentalized into others. In the 1928 work *The Young Cripple and His Job* we see a blatant example of the level of abstraction in which a physically disabled person is banned from her societal role on the basis of physical disability alone: a 1928 social worker reports the case of Elizabeth Morris, "a woman who walks with the aid of one crutch and limps only slightly," yet who was ineligible to be a school clerk solely because of her physical handicap, not because of her capability or lack thereof.[4] At the beginning of the twenty-first century, assumptions about physically disabled people are more subtly expressed. Joseph Shapiro observes the flip side of the poster child, the "supercrip," whose ordinary feats are admired out of proportion.[5]

In fact, the Greeks would not have known what to make of this discussion of physical disability. This is not to suggest that the Greeks did not notice physical disability or that physical disability did not have consequences. Rather, the consequences varied from one individual to the next and from one situation to the next, as the discussion of the Greek terminology in each chapter demonstrates. Yet ideas about disability in the ancient world are part of our common consciousness. Homer, Teiresias, and Oedipus, along with the phenomenon of Spartan infanticide of deformed infants, are often the first images that come to mind. Classicists and nonclassicists alike are quick to remember that the Greek Classical ideal included the notion of the perfectly proportioned human body and to conclude that all disabled people who varied significantly from this ideal must have been uniformly reviled. Modern assumptions that disabled people are inherently flawed, less capable, and unfortunate distort any reading of ancient historical material. One of the intents of this study is to show that able-bodiedness has unreflectively been assumed to define the essential nature of the human body and that this assumption falsely colors our interpretation of the past. The falsely colored interpretation of the past perpetuates the unreflective modern assumption that the nondisabled body is the standard against which the disabled body should be evaluated. In other words, my study reveals the distortion inherent in contemporary beliefs about disability as reflected in the portrayal of ancient Greek notions of disability. Disability in ancient Greece was treated as a family and civic issue, in which disability status was defined and negotiated between individuals on a case-by-case basis within a community, rather than as a medical one, in which what was conceived of as a "problem" was inherent in the individual. Rational medicine was in its infancy in the fifth century B.C., and for this reason if no other, disabilities were not seen as the categorizable medical phenomena that they are today.

"Physical disability" is a nebulous term. A scholarly debate over the nature of disability persists within the Society for Disability Studies, the extreme side holding that disability is entirely a cultural construction and that it does not exist intrinsically outside of any culture's definition. While I will not go that far for the purposes of this investigation, I do believe that the concept of physical disability is shaped and defined by its economic, military, political, religious, social, and technological environment. It would not make sense to approach this investigation expecting to find modern concepts and definitions of disability in the ancient world. I use modern medical terms such as "cerebral palsy," "multiple sclerosis," and "quadriplegia" for convenience, recognizing that while the medical criteria for these conditions existed in the ancient world, no ancient person would have had such medical categories in mind when observing a person with any of these diagnoses. I also use the term "physical disability" for convenience, even while I argue that no Greek would have thought about physical disability as a modern audience does.

I do not argue that the Greeks did not even notice disability or that there was a utopian continuum, with the perfectly able-bodied on one end and the totally disabled on the other, everyone else blending in a happy rainbow of varying ability. Indeed, the Greeks noticed disability, commented on it, and sometimes made fun of it in ways that would make us shudder. This does not mean that people in the ancient Greek world despised all disabled people as a class or even grouped disabled people in a class.

The "ancient Greek world" is also a nebulous term. While ancient Greek history spans the second millennium B.C. through the Roman period in the fifth century A.D., most of the surviving major historical sources are from fifth- and fourth-century B.C. Classical Greece, before the conquest of Philip II and Alexander the Great, and these centuries are the main focus of this study, though other periods are included. Furthermore, there was no "Greece"; rather, the Greek world included three or four hundred individual, autonomous city-states in various and changing alliances with each other and with their own cultural differences. The largest and most successful of these city-states in cultural, economic, and political terms was Athens, which produced the bulk of the surviving literary material.

The closest we can come to the everyday life of people with physical disabilities is by assembling a patchwork of incidental information about the political, military, economic, social, and religious consequences of disabilities. In comparison with later periods of history, not much material survives even from Athens in the Classical period. The evidence for physical disability is scattered, scant, and often contradictory. For example, no discussion of disability survives that is composed by a person who identifies himself or herself as disabled. Nevertheless, literary, papyrological, and archaeological primary sources contribute to our knowledge about disability.

The literary material includes the Hippocratic corpus, a key work in this investigation, which provides a good example of the nature of material available. The Hippocratic corpus is a compilation of material that spans the fifth through the second centuries B.C. It includes writings by the author credited with the discovery of rational medicine, Hippocrates himself, although nothing is identified securely. The corpus also includes writings by the students of Hippocrates and other medical writers. The corpus is especially valuable in that it offers an idea of the vocabulary for various conditions that we would call physical disability. Literary material, from the Homeric poems the *Iliad* and the *Odyssey,* set down in writing around the eighth century B.C., through the corpus of Galen, from the second century A.D., has been relevant. I have also used some very late literary material, such as the tenth-century encyclopedic collection that draws on earlier sources, the *Suidae Lexicon,* commonly known as the *Suda.* Although the Christian Gospels are also recorded in Greek, I omit them from my investigation because they reflect Hellenized Jewish attitudes more than Greek or even Graeco-Roman attitudes. Scholarship on disability in the Hebrew and Christian scriptures has been carried out as a separate undertaking.[6]

Documents recorded on papyrus, such as letters and legal documents, provide valuable information about daily life. Papyrological material is late in date and from Egypt, not Greece, and it is not always clear whether any given piece reflects Hellenistic (fourth through first century B.C.) or even later, Roman imperial culture. Nevertheless, the material is written in Greek and therefore has, at least, linguistic continuity. I have used papyrological material up to the sixth century A.D.

Archaeologically, Classical Greek skeletal evidence is rare. In 1946, the archaeologist J. Lawrence Angel counted the skeletal remains of eighty men and five women for all of Greece and for all periods, Neolithic through Byzantine, and concluded that it is impossible to calculate the frequency of pathology from such data. Of course, more skeletal evidence has come to light since 1946; still, the best that skeletal evidence can offer for my purposes is confirmation that various conditions existed.[7] I have used skeletal material from the Bronze Age (ca. 3000–1100 B.C.) through the eighth century A.D., in the Byzantine period, to confirm the existence of some conditions.

Because of the nature of the evidence, I paint with extremely broad strokes. There were differences, surely, between the experiences of a wealthy Athenian blind man in the Mycenaean age of powerful kings and the blind daughter of a poor island family in any period. Yet even such a huge distinction is lost, to say nothing of subtle differences. Still, some generalities can be pieced together and inferred, with the support of a wide variety of modern material. This material includes autobiographies of and poetry by people with disabilities, medical research, and theoretical works in disability studies, all of which give some shape to the scattered ancient references to disability. The physical nature of cerebral palsy has not changed over the centuries, and while there is no ancient account from a person with cerebral palsy, a modern account sheds light on everyday life in terms of physical characteristics of this disability. The humanity of disability is lost from the ancient Greek record, but poetry such as Jim Ferris's "Poems with Disabilities," the epigraph for this book, transcends time and space to express universal human experience. Poetry also makes powerful statements about common misperceptions of disability, as in the case of Lynn Manning's "The Magic Wand," in chapter 5.

Issues of disability have been very visible since the 1990s. Recent interest in disability can be seen in the political arena with the 1990 passage of and recent challenge to the Americans with Disabilities Act (ADA). The activist group Not Dead Yet framed the Kevorkian trial as an issue of disability rights. Scholarly interest in disability is also growing, as demonstrated by the interdisciplinary Society for Disability Studies, which meets annually; numerous publications such as the *Disability Studies Quarterly;* the presence of very active groups such as the Committee for Disability Issues within the Modern Language Association; graduate programs in disability studies; and Web sites such as DISC, "A Disability Studies Academic Community" (<http://www.mith2.umd.edu:8080/disc/index.html>), which represents the profusion of recent scholarship.

There has also been a growing scholarly interest in the topic of physical disability in the ancient world. Veronique Dasen couched her 1995 iconographic study of dwarfs in Greece and Egypt as a study of physical minorities.[8] Robert Garland published *The Eye of the Beholder,* a survey of deformity and disability in the Graeco-Roman world, in 1995.[9] Michael Garmaise completed his dissertation thesis, "Studies in the Representation of Dwarfs in Hellenistic and Roman Art" (McMaster University), in 1996. Daniel Ogden published *The Crooked Kings of Ancient Greece* in 1997.[10] In addition, interest in the study of the human body in the ancient world is represented by a special volume of *Arethusa,* titled *Vile Bodies: Roman Satire and Corporeal Discourse,* and by a 1999 collection edited by James Porter, *Constructions of the Classical Body.*[11]

Even some of this material suggests that disabled people in Greece were thought of as different, special, excluded, and extraordinary.[12] I argue that an inaccurate picture of disability in Greek society results from imposing the models of pity, charity, and categorization of disability onto the ancient Greek material. This study seeks to give an account of the daily realities of ordinary disabled people and investigates the persistence of our beliefs about disability in Greece.

While I limit the scope of this project to physical disability, excluding psychiatric and cognitive disorders, I also exclude two categories of physical disability in this investigation: dwarfism and epilepsy. Both categories, mostly because of their religious associations, so far transcend status as physical disabilities that they require separate investigation, and scholarly work has been done on each topic, such as the work on dwarfs mentioned earlier. On epilepsy, the classic work remains Oswei Temkin's *The Falling Sickness*.[13]

Finally, I discuss disability, not teratology. There is a difference in the Greek record between people who were physically noteworthy and people who were considered monstrous. References to blindness or lameness as descriptive markers of otherwise ordinary people do not suggest that such common conditions were considered monstrous. Aristotle describes monstrosity as the failure to resemble a human being at all (*Generation of Animals* 4.767 b 5–6). While we may not be able to determine the exact parameters of what the Greeks would have perceived as within the normal range of human variety, we can at least acknowledge that not all physical oddities would have been considered monstrous. Some of the Greeks' beloved figures, most notably Homer himself, were, in modern terms, disabled. Monstrosities such as the ones Aristotle describes (*Generation of Animals* 769 b) include aberrations such as animal heads on human bodies or humans with extra heads. Thus, in my view, the fourth-century B.C. oath that promises monstrous offspring (*terata*) to the oath breaker (Tod, *Greek Historical Inscriptions* 2:204.39–45) is not a comment about the Greeks' view of what we would term disabled people, but rather about a creature born outside the range of normal human parameters.

This book is organized into five narratives of disability in ancient Greece. The first chapter is a sketch of the Greek population in terms of its disabled element. I aim to show that the ancient Greek landscape included a wide variety of human variation, far more varied than portrayed in images of Greek perfection that are the legacy of Renaissance and Neoclassical painting. I go on to discuss daily life for people with disabilities against the modern popular idea that all "deformed" babies were killed at birth. While I do not argue that no deformed infant was ever put out to die, I point out that the lurid image of the Greeks unreflectively killing all their imperfect young is an unfounded conclusion of nineteenth-century scholars. Next, I take up the modern ideal of overcoming disability by looking at the case of Demosthenes' stutter. The fourth chapter, on deafness, continues to highlight the differences between ancient and modern understandings of disability by showing that deafness was perceived more as an intellectual impairment than as a physical disability. In the fifth chapter, I challenge the notion that blindness was always a horror or a blessing—or both—and that we can even speak of ancient and modern blindness in the same way. I conclude by challenging the translation of the term "unable" (*adunatos*) as "disabled," with all its modern associations.

While many of my colleagues have made the switch to B.C.E. ("before the common era") and C.E. ("common era"), I persist in using B.C. ("before Christ") and A.D. ("anno domini," "the year of our Lord"). It seems to me that the B.C.E./C.E. system adds yet another layer of artificiality and Christian-centricism to an already artificial and Christian-centric system of dating (after all, we do not know precisely when Jesus was born, and people had no idea that they were living in the B.C. era).[14] The "common era" in B.C.E./C.E. dating corresponds to the supposed birth of Christ—there's nothing else common about it—and thus, using B.C.E./C.E. seems to me to highlight, rather than downplay, the already artificial and Christian-centric system.

1   The Landscape of Disability ❧

Our mental image of the ancient Greek landscape is shaped by indelible literary and artistic Renaissance and Neoclassical depictions of the idealized Greek physical form. Johann Joachim Winckelmann, the eighteenth-century scholar of art history, wrote that

> the most beautiful body of ours would perhaps be as much inferior to the most beautiful Greek one. . . . The forms of the Greeks, prepared to beauty, by the influence of the mildest and purest sky, became perfectly elegant by their early exercises.[1]

This image is immortalized in the visual imagery of Renaissance painting, for example, Raphael's *School of Athens,* in which perfectly proportioned bodies gather around perfectly proportioned buildings (see fig. 1).[2] Such visual imagery is continued in Neoclassical painting, such as David's *Death of Socrates.* In both cases, even Socrates—whose physical form, ironically, is described as ugly in the historical sources (e.g., in Plato *Symposium* 215 a–b)—is painted in perfect proportion.

In fact, the ancient Greek world was inhabited by people with a wide range of visible physical disabilities. In any given public gathering place, one would have seen a much greater variety of physical conditions than one would see in the developed world today. This variety of physical forms would have included not only the beautiful bodies of Winckelmann's conjecture but also children affected by clubfoot and rickets, people with spastic cerebral palsy, disabled war veterans, and people with a host of other somatic variations. The physical environ-

The Renaissance image of Classical Greece: perfectly proportioned bodies are arranged in harmony with perfectly proportioned buildings. Raphael, *School of Athens*, 1510. Fresco in the Stanza della Segnatura, Palazzi Vaticani, Rome. Scala/Art Resource, N.Y.

ment in which these people lived differed vastly from Renaissance and Neoclassical depictions and from the modern, developed world. Not only the physical but also the cultural environment—the environment of attitudes—differed significantly from that of the modern, developed world, as I will argue here and in subsequent chapters.

As a preliminary to discussion of what physical disability meant to the Greeks, it is useful to consider first the varieties of physical disability. Following a brief discussion of the vocabulary for physical disability, a catalog of the physical handicaps that existed in the ancient Greek world highlights the differences between the ancient and modern profiles of physical disability and suggests that physical impairment was common in the ancient world. This suggestion comes as no surprise, since vaccines and antibiotics as we know them today did not exist in the ancient world. Furthermore, a catalog of the many physical impairments is a corrective to the image of the perfect Greek human body that has been left to us in Greek statuary and fortified by erroneous artistic depictions of everyday Greek life. In this chapter, I limit the discussion to physical conditions that affect the limbs. I deal with conditions leading to blindness, deafness, and speech disorders in separate chapters.

Although there is an extensive list of Greek terms that describe conditions of being maimed, blind, and so on, there is no Greek equivalent for the modern, overarching term "disabled," with its many social and political connotations. Permanent physical disability was not the concern of doctors in antiquity beyond recognition of incurability, and the vocabulary for physical disability appears vague, at best, to the modern audience. References to permanent physical handicaps are scattered throughout nearly all the literary material, but handicaps did not belong in the domain of rational medicine, which treated curable diseases; in fact, a Hippocratic practitioner's ability to distinguish an incurable case as opposed to a curable one was part of his skill.[3] The Greek terms for physical impairment are general and describe outward appearances or symptoms; in contrast, we in the developed world are accustomed to technical, medical categorizations of specific physical conditions. Inherent in a modern term such as "cerebral palsy" or "muscular dystrophy," for example, is the etiology, range of symptoms, prognosis, and so on. In the ancient world, the term "maimed" or "formless" implied a varied range of conditions, so a Greek would form a mental picture of a maimed or formless person, but not an accompanying etiology or prognosis. The difference, though, is that the image intended by any given term varied from usage to usage, informed by the context and by the public reading or performance. We have only the written terms, for the most part. Without the context, the specifics of the terms are usually lost, to say nothing of subtle shifts in meaning between audiences and over time. It is also important to note that no term refers exclusively to physical impairment. Most of the terms are part of a general vocabulary as opposed to a medical vocabulary, and the terms are generic, even interchangeable, taking on specific meaning only in the individual contexts in which they were used.[4] It is also important to note that none of these terms refers exclusively to human physical impairment. Theophrastus, a fourth- and third-century B.C. botanist, for example, uses "maimed" (*pepêrô-menon*) to refer to parts of plants (*On the Causes of Plants* 3.5.1).

Nevertheless, it is useful to set out some general definitions, along with a sense of each term's extreme breadth. "Maimed" (*pêros*) and all its variations—such as "much-maimed" (*anapêros*)—is an extremely general term for any body that deviated significantly in outward appearance from the standard. We can sense the huge breadth of this term when, writing in the fourth century B.C., Aristotle refers to the "deformity" (*pêrôsis*) of baldness (*Generation of Animals* 784 a) but also refers to monstrosity as the state of being very disfigured (*anapêria*) (*Generation of Animals* 769 b). The term was used to describe everyone from Thamyris, whom, the eighth-century B.C. Homeric writings tell us, the Muses maimed (*cholôsamentai pêron thesan*) because he boasted that his musical skills were as great as theirs (*Iliad* 2.599), to Aristotle's speculation (*Generation of Animals* 737 a) that a female is technically a deformed (*pepêrômenôn*) male. Herodotus, the fifth-century historian and chronicler of the Persian Wars, uses this most broad term when he has the wisest man in the world say that the fortunate man is the one who ends his life "without disfigurement [*apêros*], sickness, or evil" (1.32).

Another term that sometimes describes people with physical handicaps usually means "disgrace," but also "ugliness" (*aischos;* also *aischros,* "ugly"). Thersites' limp, his rounded shoulders, and his bald head add up to an overall appearance of the ugliest man (*aischistos de anêr*) among the Greek forces in the Trojan War (Homer *Iliad* 2.216). While the detailed description of Thersites' ugliness paints a distinctive appearance, what Plato had in mind specifically when he discusses a crude form of dance that imitates the movements of ugly people (*ais-chionôn*) is anyone's guess (*Laws* 7.814).[5] The term is also used in a very general sense when Plato, writing in the fourth century B.C., has Socrates contrast weakness (*asthenountes*) with health (*hugiainontes*) (*Alcibiades* 2.139 a).

"Weakness" (*astheneia*) also leaves much to the modern imagination. An author in the Hippocratic corpus, for example, describes weakness as a symptom of a certain withering disease (*auantê*) in which the legs become weak and heavy and the patient wastes away (*Diseases* 2.66). The term is also used throughout the Hippocratic corpus as a general term for sickness (e.g., *Ancient Medicine* 12, 13; *Regimen in Acute Diseases* 11). Aristotle uses the term in a similar way when he warns that the children of both too-young and too-old parents are imperfect (*ateleis*) and weak (*asthenês*) in body (*Politics* 1335 a–b).

"Incompleteness" or "imperfection" (*ateleia*) sometimes refers to physical handicaps, such as when the biographer Plutarch (ca. A.D. 50–120) describes the child of Isis and Osiris, born "weak in his lower limbs" (*asthenê tois katôthen guiois*) (*Moralia* 358 e). Aristotle also uses the term to refer to children who were born imperfectly (*atelê*), but in this case, it refers to a far less severe condition, in which passages in infants' ears or nostrils are not fully formed but correct themselves in time (*Generation of Animals* 775 a).

"Maimed" or "mutilated" (*kolobos*) is a general but fairly unambiguous term that can refer to physical impairment. Aristotle plainly states that the term can only refer to an object or a body that is missing something, such as a vessel missing a handle or a person missing an irreplaceable extremity (*Metaphysics* 5.27.3–4 1024 a). Thus Plutarch paints the paradox of a mutilated man (*kolobou*) fearing he will become hundred-handed (*Moralia* 93.1 c).

The meaning of "lameness" (*cholos*) is a straightforward reference to lameness in the leg. Plutarch writes that each body part has its own weakness: the eye is prone to blindness; the leg is prone to lameness (*chôlotêta*) (*Moralia* 963 c–d). Within this specific definition, though, the range of application is enormous. Plutarch, for example, uses the same term to refer to both the Spartan king Agesilaus, whose limp was so slight that it was barely noticeable (*Agesilaus* 2.2–3), and to a man who could not walk at all (*Pericles* 27.3–4).

"Unable" (*adunatos*) is potentially a dangerously misleading term, because it is so close in meaning and sense to the modern "disabled," with all its political and cultural associations. There are crucial differences between the Greek "unable" and the modern "disabled," differences that I discuss in this book's conclusion. The Greek term is literal and is seen in many situations in which one is not able to accomplish something. Herodotus, for example, uses the same term, "unable" (*adunatoi*), in the context of a group of people who are unable to persuade another group of people (3.138) and to describe ships that had been disabled (6.16).

Any population, ancient or modern, includes people with physical handicaps, but medical science has altered the profile of types of physical disability. On one hand, there are people with disabilities in the modern world who would not have survived in the ancient world. People have been able to survive spinal-cord injury, for example, only since the 1960s; survival of injury high in the spinal cord, which implies paralysis from the shoulders down, only became possible in recent decades. On the other hand, the ancient world included people with physical handicaps that are not commonly seen today in the developed world, such as clubfoot, broken bones that have not healed properly, and the effects of epidemic diseases such as tuberculosis.[6]

The following catalog of physical handicaps likely to be found in an ancient Greek population is organized along the life cycle, beginning with a discussion of congenital physical handicaps. A survey of physical handicaps resulting from injury and disease is followed by some remarks on several disabling conditions such as cerebral palsy and multiple sclerosis. I close by mentioning the disabling conditions that might accompany old age.

From the standpoint of modern science, congenital handicaps result from three categories of causes: heredity, the circumstances of gestation, and the conditions of birth. The Greeks also observed that one might be born with an "inherited" physical handicap in imitation of one's parents. Aristotle observes that physically impaired children are born of physically impaired parents; for example, lame parents sometimes produce lame children (*History of Animals* 585 b, 586 a). Also, Aristotle observes that mutilated children are born of mutilated parents (*Generation of Animals* 721 b). The Roman scholar Pliny echoes this observation five centuries later: lame children, he writes, are born from lame parents (*Natural History* 7.11.50). Such births were common enough for Pseudo-Aristotle, an anonymous student of Aristotle whose work was traditionally ascribed to Aristotle, to ask why it is more common for the human being than any other animal to be born lame (*Problems* 895 a). Several centuries before Aristotle, Greek audiences heard the blacksmith god Hephaestus blaming his parents for his lameness, and thus for Aphrodite's preference for the war god Ares, in Homer's *Odyssey* (8.308–12):

> Yet for this is none other to blame but my two parents—would they had never begotten me![7]

In later tradition, two sons of Hephaestus were lame. Apollonius Rhodius, the third-century B.C. author of the *Argonautica*, explains that Palaemonius was born of Hephaestus and because of this (*tounek'*) his feet were crippled (*Argonautica* 1.202–6). Apollodorus (3.16.1) tells the tale of Periphites, another son of Hephaestus, who had weak feet (*podas de astheneis*). A Hippocratic author observes that lameness lies in heredity (*Sacred Disease* 3). Of course, ancient scholars were not equipped to understand the differences between birth defects caused by heredity on the one hand and chromosomal aberration on the other, but simply recorded their observations. So Aristotle also remarks that children sometimes inherit such characteristics as scars and brands (*Generation of Animals* 724 a).[8]

Circumstances of gestation constitute another category of congenital physical disability. Impairments such as spinal malformation and clubfoot can be acquired in the womb regardless of genetic configurations.[9] In the United States today, one in one thousand children are born each year with clubfoot.[10] Again, while ancient observers had no way to distinguish what was genetically determined and what was a result of the mother's inadequate nutrition, for example, they did guess that a baby could acquire a deformity during the period of gestation and as a result of the circumstances of gestation. A mother's inadequate nutrition was a significant factor in the ancient world in terms of producing offspring with physical anomalies.[11] Aristotle observes that babies might be born with too many or too few parts, such as toes, as a result of the "setting" process of gestation, which can also result in unusually large hands or feet, or several of them (*Generation of Animals* 772 b). Further, he explains that offspring might be born without an extremity, as a result of a small abortion of that particular extremity (*Generation of Animals* 773 a).[12]

The conditions of birth constitute the third cause of congenital deformity. Even if a fetus were to grow unharmed in the womb, its birth might be premature. While Plutarch is not discussing physiology in his tale of Isis and Osiris, it is interesting that he blames the untimely birth of their son, Harpocrates, for his unfinished body (*Moralia* 377 c, 378 c). Specifically, he describes Harpocrates' unfinished body as having "weakness in his lower limbs" (*Moralia* 358 e). Pseudo-Aristotle answers his own query about why it is more common for man than any other animal to be born lame by explaining that men have many seasons of birth, including the seventh, eighth, and tenth months of pregnancy (*Problems* 895 a). Aristotle writes that seven-month children are born imperfectly but that many survive (*Generation of Animals* 775 a).[13] Prematurely born babies are, in fact, at risk for physical impairment such as cerebral palsy and motor incoordination.[14]

Children born without a handicap could acquire one from a variety of circumstances later in life. Permanent physical disability could result from injured, diseased, and lost limbs; from diseases such as arthritis; and from several other conditions. Some Greeks believed that physical handicaps might result from additional factors such as curses. We see a possible example of this in an inscribed curse from the fifth century B.C., in which the victim is cursed to fall from sickness into permanent handicap.[15] Another sort of curse was the evil eye, the belief that some people can inflict harm by looking at other people or their property.[16] Protective devices against the evil eye, still in use all over the world today, have a long tradition. One of the earliest protective devices used by the Greeks was the head of the Gorgon.[17]

With or without the influence of magic, even the most minor injury could have permanent consequences. Accidents or events causing fractures were common. Whether as a result of improper healing or as the result of infection, fractured and dislocated bones were likely to result in a permanent physical handicap in the ancient world. In the developed world, we take for granted that, with medical attention, even the most severe fracture will be undetectably repaired. Without medical attention, fractures sometimes spontaneously and completely heal, but not always. There is evidence in a male from the Middle Bronze Age (second millennium B.C.) of a right humerus fracture with a resulting fifteen-degree angulation and shortening of the bone. In another male, from the Protogeometric period (the twelfth through eighth centuries B.C.), a fracture of the left tibia shaft resulted in five-degree angulation and shortening, and in a male from the Hellenistic period (323–146

B.C.), a fracture of the left femur angled twenty degrees and thickened.[18]

A simple accident, such as a fall, could have irreversible consequences in the ancient world. A Hippocratic writer explains that people who leap down from a height and land violently on the heel will separate the bones and risk necrosis and gangrene (*On Fractures* 11). Concern over permanent impairment takes on mythical proportions in the tale of the god Hephaestus, whose lameness was connected, in some versions, with his long fall from the heavens to the earth.[19] Herodotus tells us that the Persian ruler Darius, having dislocated his foot in the process of dismounting from his horse, gave up hope of ever using the foot again, and this despite having the best doctors (3.129–30). This passage is not straightforward testimony, of course. Rather, Herodotus tells the story as a showcase for the art of Greek medicine.[20] Nevertheless, it had to ring true among Greek audiences. A similar example, of a humbler person, Cephesias, comes from a fourth-century B.C. dedicatory inscription at the healing site of Epidaurus, the domain of the healing god Asclepius. Cephesias had been thrown from his horse, and his foot was maimed, to the point that he had to be carried into the temple. Cephesias was said to have received this injury as divine punishment because he had laughed at the Asclepiadic cures for lameness, and he was cured only after he recanted.[21]

While it is assumed in the developed world that medical attention to a broken bone will result in its healing, a visit from a doctor in Classical Greece could have a range of possible results. In the ancient world, a doctor's training was not standardized, licensed, or necessarily respected. As a Hippocratic writer warns, some doctors, through their showy bandagings, do the patient more harm than good (*On Fractures* 1). We read instructions for reduction—restoring a bone to its normal position—which, in most cases, could only have caused further damage (*On Fractures* 13). A broken thigh bone that results in a shortened thigh because of faulty medical treatment, we are told, is evidence of poor medical judgment. It is not clear if the writer is giving literal advice or simply making a point when he advises the physician that it is better to break both legs and at least have them in equilibrium (*On Fractures* 19).[22] The second-century A.D. physician Galen, who continued and elaborated many aspects of Hippocratic rational medicine in the Roman world, also describes elaborate methods of reduction (13.333–34, 18b.400–404). There was no standard medical treatment for any given malady, but rather a variety of treatment methods. Some treatments seem sound; others seem of dubious value to the modern eye. For example, Galen was in favor of letting blood as a remedy for injured limbs (5.118–19, inter alia).

Even if a bone is tended to and set properly, it must remain immobilized to effect complete healing. While animals with broken bones do this by instinct, the need to tend a shop or a field would probably override any human instinct to remain idle. In fact, a Hippocratic writer notes that while a patient with a broken foot should remain immobile for twenty days, "patients, despising the injury, do not bring themselves to do this, but go about before they are well" (*On Fractures* 9).[23] Also relevant is a passage from the Hippocratic corpus that states that when the bones are not completely regenerated, the hip, thigh, and leg gradually become atrophied and that when recuperation is prevented, the limbs become convex or concave and there is shortening of the bone (*On Fractures* 14, 16). A Hippocratic writer notes that fractured bones tend to become distorted during the mending (*On Fractures* 8). Of a certain kind of bone displacement in the leg, we read a warning that the doctor should know that such injured people will be lame (*On Joints* 63). A dislocated bone or one that has healed crookedly can be reduced, but the reduction of broken bones is difficult even in modern times, mostly because of the muscle spasms that accompany the procedure. The procedure also requires proper anesthetics, unavailable in the ancient world.[24]

Some war wounds would leave men permanently physically handicapped.[25] An ancient Greek audience would have known that Eurypylus, limping back from the battlefield with a wound in his thigh, was in serious danger (Homer *Iliad* 11.809–11). The immediate measures taken by his companion Patroclus may indeed have killed the pain and stopped the flow of blood (Homer *Iliad* 11.842–48), but an injury to the femur, the largest bone in the body, leads to complications such as torn muscles and long-lasting infections. Indeed, a Hippocratic writer reports that the fractured thighbone will lead to a shortened thigh (*On Fractures* 19) and that the thighbone distorts easily (*On Fractures* 20). There is, of course, a wide range of additional war injuries that would have led to permanent physical handicaps if the injured person had survived. The paleopathologist Srboljub Živanović writes that "the morphological deformities that arose are really beyond imagination at the present time."[26]

Permanently irregular gait was so common that a Hippocratic author cataloged the varieties of gait. In the case of a certain type of hip dislocation, for example, the patients "have an even swaying gait to this side and that" (*On Joints* 56). Patients with another sort of hip dislocation might "keep the leg raised and contracted, and walk on the other, supporting themselves, some with one and some with two crutches" (*On Joints* 58). Adults with dislocated thighs "keep the whole leg straighter in walking," and "sometimes they drag the foot along the ground" (*On Joints* 60).

However one treated a bone injury, it was not just the injured bone, but rather the infection that might ensue, that was responsible for extreme damage. A Greek would have been lucky if the bone simply healed crookedly, because every bone injury was also susceptible to infection.[27] Untreated by antibiotics, an infection can spread throughout the surrounding tissues, then the bone itself, attacking even the bone marrow. In Sophocles' tragedy *Philoctetes,* the stench of Philoctetes' wound, which had festered for ten years, was a literary device, certainly, but surely familiar to the fifth-century B.C. Athenian audience and drawn from direct observation of a festering wound.[28] Neoptolemus and Odysseus, Greek soldiers of the Trojan War who are looking for Philoctetes on his island of exile, find evidence of his presence:

> *Neoptolemus:* Aha! Here's something else! Yes, some rags drying in the
> sun. They're reeking with matter from some terrible sore. (*Philoctetes*
> 38–39)[29]

If the injured person survived severe infection, the necrotic bones could become extremely deformed, not just at the injury but around the whole area.[30] Some limbs did not heal at all but, diseased, fell off. Ischemia (localized anemia) and gangrene (decay of tissue resulting from this lack of blood supply) are common results of injury.[31] Limb loss could also result from ischemia and gangrene from advanced diabetes. While inherited diabetes is probably as old as the human race, it is not identified by the Hippocratic writers, although it does appear in the writings of Celsus, a first-century A.D. Roman author who assembled Hellenistic medical knowledge, and in the writings of Galen.[32] We hear, too, of frostbite and consequent loss of fingers, toes, and limbs of soldiers in cold countries from the fourth-century military historian

Xenophon (*Anabasis* 7.4.3); the first-century B.C. historian Diodorus (3.34.2, 14.28.3); and Lucian, from the second century A.D. (*The Ignorant Book-Collector* 6). Cold injuries have been documented at surprisingly warm temperatures, up to twelve degrees Celsius, or about fifty-four degrees Fahrenheit. The limbs do not fall off immediately from the cold, but rather mummify and fall off on their own or can be removed with forceps a few weeks later. In frostbite injury, the deep damage is not recognizable from the external injury and sometimes is not discovered until months or years later.[33] Limb loss was enough of a concern that Diodorus's utopian island (2.58.4–5) included the feature of limb reattachment: the blood of a certain tortoiselike animal is used, he tells us, to glue back on severed limbs; of course, the cut must be fresh and the severed part not a vital part.

It is safe to assume that gangrene led to a wide variety of outcomes in a world without antibiotics. Today, minor amputation can forestall or prevent major limb amputation, and no amputation necessarily means death by infection, as a range of antibiotics is now prescribed for the healing process. Preventative amputation seems not to have been practiced during the Classical period. In the Hippocratic corpus, amputation is always a passive matter; that is, the limb falls off on its own or is pulled off only when it is ready to come away anyway. We learn from Hippocratic writers the details of when and how the necrotic bones might fall off. We read, for example, that "the more porous bones come away more quickly, the more solid more slowly" (*On Fractures* 33). Similarly, in *Prognostic,* the author observes that when a patient's fingers and feet are blackened, the patient will lose the blackened parts (9). It is difficult to determine exactly when amputation became a medical practice; it could have existed all along as a sort of barbershop service. Plato implies that amputation has become an active matter by the time of his writing in the fourth century B.C., rather than a passive one of waiting for the bone to fall off, when he makes an analogy stating that men are prepared to have hands and feet cut off, if they believe that they are harmful (*Symposium* 205 e). Of course, he may have been exaggerating. Plutarch, writing five centuries after Plato, is more specific about amputation when he makes his analogy: he writes that when one's foot or hand is mortified, one pays to have it cut off (*Moralia* 831 d).[34] By Celsus's time, amputation is taken for granted and must have been practiced by the Hellenistic Alexandrians.[35] In any case, people with missing limbs were common enough that Aristotle could include as an example of artful refutation that "biped" is not truly a property of man, because not every man is in possession of two feet (*Topics* 134 a).

In addition to injury and infection, disease could be responsible for permanent physical impairment. Osteoarthritis, the degenerative joint disease, is, in the United States today, second only to cardiovascular disease as a cause of chronic disability among adults.[36] Osteoarthritis was present in the ancient world, estimated by J. Lawrence Angel to have occurred at an 8 to 15 percent frequency in the general ancient Greek population.[37] There is evidence of arthritis in skeletons ranging from the Sub-Mycenaean through the Hellenistic period (i.e., from ca. 1100 B.C. through the second century B.C.).[38] Rheumatoid arthritis, a chronic, inflammatory disorder of the connective tissue that today affects three million Americans, also existed in the ancient world.[39] Rheumatoid arthritis is incurable, but its symptoms are handled today with a range of treatments, such as steroid drugs and surgery, that were not available in the ancient world. Gout, too, was recognized and discussed by the Hippocratics.[40] The skeleton of a female from the Protogeometric period shows signs of a big-toe inflammation, a common symptom of gout.[41] Gout can be kept under control today by a variety of drugs; while we do not know the specifics, people suffering from gout in the ancient world also had treatments available.[42] Infectious arthritis is not a well-known phenomenon in the modern world, as it can be treated with antibiotics; sterile treatment for injuries has led to fewer cases of infectious arthritis. In the ancient world, however, infectious arthritis developed freely and led to major destruction of the joints.[43]

Possible portrayals of people affected by arthritis appear in the literature. Hesiod, critiquing Archaic Greek society around 700 B.C., describes the "three-legged One, whose back is broken and whose head looks down upon the ground" (*Works and Days* 533–35). This image could be based on the common sight of a man with osteoarthritis; the "swollen foot with a shrunk hand" could describe the effects of gout (*Works and Days* 497).[44] A man who visited the temple of Asclepius because of a severely sore toe, and who left dedicatory thanks for his cure, may have been experiencing gout.[45] Another example of a passage that could refer to arthritic limbs or other disease-related conditions is Aristotle's example of youthful hyperbole, "legs twisted like parsley" (*Rhetoric* 1413 a). Also, Xenophon compares the gait of horses to that of a twisted-legged man, saying that horses with flat hooves tread with the strongest and weakest parts of the foot simultaneously (*Art of Horsemanship* 1.3).

Epidemic diseases could leave whole groups of people with permanent physical handicaps. A Hippocratic writer observes an epidemic of erysipelas—literally, "red skin," an acute streptococcal disease of the skin and subcutaneous tissue that spreads—in which the flesh and sinews fell away. "Many," he reports, "lost the arm and the entire forearm" (*Epidemics* 3.4). Thucydides, the historian who chronicled the Peloponnesian War at the end of the fifth century B.C., reports the loss of extremities due to the plague of 429 B.C. (2.49.8).[46] This Athenian plague was unique only in its careful documentation; there were other plagues.[47] Tuberculosis, for example, occurs in epidemics.[48] While we have no direct written evidence for the crippling results of tuberculosis, we do have paleopathological evidence of its results in the ancient world.[49] Bone and joint tuberculosis causes various bone changes; for example, paraplegia can develop from spinal tuberculosis.[50] A certain Hermodicus was "paralyzed in body," whether by tuberculosis or some other condition (*ACIT* 232–33). In the modern world, we think of impairments in terms of their medical cause; in the ancient world, such medical compartmentalization was not standard.

In addition to congenital handicaps; injured, diseased, and lost limbs; and the results of diseases such as arthritis, we can conjecture the presence of other conditions associated with physical impairment even if the details are irretrievable. Cerebral palsy, for example, must have existed—it results from brain damage during gestation or birth—even though we have no written medical acknowledgment of it. A sketch of brain damage at birth might be seen when Aristotle describes the birth of babies who appear bloodless and dead, but whom skilled midwives can revive (*History of Animals* 587 a). An inscription from Epidaurus (*ACIT* 237) describes a man "paralyzed in the knees," which could describe the gait of cerebral palsy; of course, it could also describe a number of other maladies. We see a possible portrayal of cerebral palsy in a Hellenistic sculpture of the head of a man with facial asymmetry.[51] Pseudo-Aristotle's "morbid character" typifies a person affected by cerebral palsy: "weak-eyed, knock-kneed, his head inclined to right, his palm upward or slack, and he has two gaits: he either waggles hips or holds them stiffly" (*Physiognomics* 808 a). Similarly, although the effects of cerebral palsy were not recognized per se, perhaps it was the visual image of a person with spastic cerebral palsy that Herodotus had in mind when he relates that when men or animals passed by the site of the murdered Phoecaeans they "became distorted and crippled and palsied" (*apoplêkta,* literally, "stricken") (1.167).

Multiple sclerosis is a disease of the central nervous system white matter that causes symptoms in the brain, spinal cord, and optic nerves. Greece lies within the medium zone of prevalence of multiple sclerosis; that is, there are between five and thirty people in ten thousand with multiple sclerosis in Greece today.[52] A similar incidence in the ancient world cannot be ruled out; the etiology of multiple sclerosis is unproven. We may see the unpredictable and episodic symptoms of multiple sclerosis in the second-century B.C. series of decrees honoring Archippe, a benefactress who seems to have had recurring bouts of weakness followed by health (*SEG* 33.1035–41).

Malnutrition, too, was responsible for some physical impairments.[53] The bones of children who were underfed would not have had a chance to develop properly. While very little is known about the feeding of infants in ancient Greece, cereals were probably a common supplement for children.[54] This diet would have led to protein deficiency and was probably associated with poverty, as it is now.[55] Vitamin deficiencies, especially in combination with swaddling, likely led to such malformations as rickets.[56] Malnutrition in general was common in all young children, even those of the rich.[57]

Cardiovascular accident (CVA, or "stroke") can result in permanent physical impairment. A Hippocratic writer describes the symptoms quite clearly, even if he attributes them to certain weather conditions: old men, he observes, become paralyzed in their right or left side *(Airs Waters Places* 10). Aristotle may describe the symptoms of CVA as well when he uses as a simile "the case of paralysis" in which when one "wills to move his limbs to the right they swerve to the left" (*Nicomachean Ethics* 1.13.16). Galen describes hemiplegia following damage to either the right or the left side of the brain (8.230).

Several additional conditions probably existed in the ancient world, such as the results of cancers, spina bifida, post-polio syndrome, and brain trauma.[58] While it is out of the scope of this discussion to detail each condition, they round out this catalog of the possible types of physical impairment likely to have been present.

Finally, equating old age and physical weakness is common in Greek literature.[59] Old age is associated with physical infirmity from the earliest Greek literary record. The prototype of the old soldier, Nestor, acknowledges his old age by pointing out his physical characteristics (Homer *Iliad* 23.627–28):

> My limbs are no longer steady, dear friend; nor my feet, neither do my arms, as once they did, swing light from my shoulders.[60]

We see the equation of old age and stiff limbs in fifth-century comedy. Aristophanes has the chorus of Acharnians, neighbors to the Athenians in Attica, identify themselves as old men by cataloging their physical woes: "Now because my joints have stiffened / and my shins are young no more" (*Acharnians* 219–21).[61] The solution to the riddle of the Sphinx depends upon an understanding that old men use canes with which to walk just as surely as all babies crawl. Aeschylus alludes to the riddle of the Sphinx in the tragedy *Agamemnon:* "extreme old age walks on three feet" (79–80). Pliny remarks that "the senses grow dull, the limbs are numb, and the sight, hearing, gait, and teeth die before we do" (*Natural History* 7.50.168). The reverse of reality is seen in the inhabitants of a utopian island in Diodorus's imagination who live 150 years in perfect health; anyone who becomes impaired must, by law, commit suicide (2.57.5).

Thus, the ancient Greek population included a substantial portion of people with permanent physical handicaps. There were many conditions that would have resulted in a physical handicap, several of which have been controlled or eliminated in the modern, developed world.

Mobility is another factor in the landscape of disability. People who were missing limbs or who had other significant mobility impairments probably got around as best they could, using crutches if necessary. There is absolutely no evidence for the wheelchair, today's universal symbol of disability and favorable parking spots. Nor is there evidence for small carts on which people could propel themselves. A Hippocratic writer describes young children with dislocated limbs who "crawl about on the sound leg," supporting themselves with the hand on the sound side on the ground, and indicates that some adults crawl around as well (*On Joints* 52).[62] For distances, the ancient equivalent of a wheelchair was probably the donkey, such as Hephaestus rides in the depictions of his return to Olympus (see fig. 2; note that the god's feet are turned backward).[63] This transportation perhaps produced the slightly obscene expression, "the lame man rides best" (Mimnermus

Hephaestus rides the ancient equivalent of the wheelchair. Note that his feet are turned backward in this early sixth-century depiction. *Hephaestus' Return,* first quarter of the sixth century B.C., Corinth. National Archaeological Museum, Athens. Cat. number 664 (CC 628). Reproduced with permission from the National Archaeological Museum, Athens.

frag. 23; Athenaeus 13.568 e).[64] People who could not walk, temporarily or permanently, could be transported in carts, presumably, though we only see people who were able to walk carried in carts, such as the ox cart (e.g., Herodotus 1.31). Litters were also available for transporting the sick and the injured, as well as people permanently unable to walk, such as those who were carried into the Asclepiadic temple at Epidaurus (*ACIT* 236). Artemon, a lame (*chôlon*) siege-engine designer, was also carried in a litter (Plutarch *Pericles* 27.3–4).

People who could walk but who had difficulty walking probably used staffs or canes. As Plutarch puts it, the lame man makes no progress without his stick (*Moralia* 922 b). Plutarch explains that Hephaestus is associated with fire because he would make no progress without his cane, just as fire makes no progress without wood.[65] We see another example of a lame man (*chôlos*) with his stick on a fourth-century B.C. stele at Epidaurus (*ACIT* 233.) Indeed, the staff was an emblem of the unsteady feet of the old, part of Odysseus's disguise as a hobbling beggar (Homer *Odyssey* 17.203, 336–38).

While a slight limp does not impede progress very much, a missing foot, for example, makes mobility quite difficult.[66] In addition to crutches or staffs, apparently there were other aids for people who had difficulty walking, such as the corrective boots and shoes mentioned incidentally in the Hippocratic corpus (*On Joints* 62). Plutarch may have such a boot in mind in his story of Damonidas the music master, who prays, when he loses his boots, specially made for his crippled feet, that they might fit their finder (*Moralia* 18 d).[67]

Prosthetic devices are not mentioned at all in the Hippocratic corpus. The scraps of evidence that survive indicate that prosthetic aids were individually crafted items, not medically prescribed implements.[68] Herodotus tells us that Hegesistratus, the diviner on the staff of the Persian general Mardonius, forced to cut off his own foot in order to escape from a Spartan prison, fashioned a prosthetic foot out of wood (9.37).[69] Lucian tells the tale of a man who, having lost his feet to frostbite, strapped on wooden feet and hobbled with the help of servants (*The Ignorant Book-Collector* 6). Pliny relates the story of the Roman general Sergius, who, having lost his right hand, has a very unlikely prosthetic hand made of iron (*Natural History* 7.28.104–5). It is difficult to believe that any prosthetic device would have been practical as well as cosmetic. Even today, with advanced understanding of pre-prosthetic preparation and a wide array of prosthetic choices, prosthetic devices are often discarded because of the great energy expenditure that it takes to use them.[70] Additional complications from prosthetic devices can result, such as limited use of other parts of the body and skin problems, even in properly fitted prosthetic devices.[71]

An archaeological example confirms that wooden prosthetic devices existed in the ancient world: an artificial leg of wood, covered with bronze sheathing, was found on a skeleton from Capua, from about

300 B.C.[72] While this is the only archaeological example of a true artificial limb from the Classical period, there is an example from mythology: Pelops's shoulder, after it was mistakenly eaten as part of the stew that his father, Tantalus, served to the gods, was replaced by one of ivory.[73]

The institution is another difference between the modern and ancient landscapes of disability. For better or worse, nursing homes and other institutions have been the homes—or warehouses, depending on one's perspective—of disabled people who are unable to carry out their own daily living independently. By contrast, the ancient state was not involved in the care of such people.

Even if some war veterans were maintained by the state at Athens, as Plutarch suggests (*Solon* 31), the maintenance was a small monetary amount, and no provision for physical care was made.[74] Physical care for an ordinary handicapped person was a family matter.[75] A letter from the fourth century A.D., though admittedly late and from a man who is injured, not necessarily permanently physically handicapped, illustrates both the difficulty faced by people unable to care for themselves and the reliance on one's family for physical care. The writer, Judas, has had a riding accident and is in Babylon, far from his home in Egypt: "For when I want to turn on to my other side, I cannot do it by myself, unless two other persons turn me over, and I have no one to give me so much as a cup of water" (8–11). The writer goes on to ask the recipient of the letter, his sister, to travel to him (16) (*P. Oxy.* 46.3314). We can only guess at the range of conditions that must have existed for physically handicapped people who required physical assistance, but we do not have any direct information. The surviving literature shows us only the extremes of solicitousness and neglect and only the case of old or ill people, not permanently physically handicapped people. On one hand, the legendary models of devotion, Cleobis and Biton, were so dutiful that they yoked a cart to themselves in order to transport their old mother (Herodotus 1.31). In contrast, in a third-century B.C. petition, a man complains that although he is stricken with bodily infirmity and failing eyesight, his daughter won't care for him in his old age (*Sel. Pap.* 2.268). We also get a glimpse of at least one person's attitude to caring for a family member—again, not a physically handicapped family member, but rather an old and sick one—in a speech of the fourth-century Athenian rhetor Isocrates. Isocrates has helped his client argue for the right to the inheritance of his father by describing the drudgery of caring for him when he lay bedridden for six months (*Aegineticus* 24–29).[76]

People who were unable to care for themselves were not routinely segregated from the public, but part of the family and the community. This is not to say that the Greeks should be taken as humanitarians who practiced mainstreaming before their time; indeed, some families, then as now, may have abused, locked away, or killed family members who became burdensome. Assuming that this was the exception and not the rule, people with a wide variety of physical disabilities were a normal part of the human landscape. As the epigraph for this book suggests, disabled people are always in our midst, and we are all potentially disabled. Acknowledging that disability was significant in the Greek population gives rise to questions about the social, economic, religious, and military status of people with disabilities, discussed in the next chapter.

2 Killing Defective Babies ∿

The Greeks practiced exposure, the discarding of unwanted infants. The story of Oedipus, as central a legend to the Greeks as the story of Cinderella is to us, rests on the assumption that unwanted babies were put out to die. Oedipus's ankles were pierced and he was exposed to the elements to die on the orders of his father, because his patricide had been foretold. The story of Oedipus, though, does *not* rest on the assumption that *all* deformed babies were put out to die. It is possible that the name Oedipus (Oidipous) is a play on words and means "swollen-foot" (*oideô pous*), referring to the permanent injuries that Oedipus received from his ankles being pierced at birth. In conversation (as opposed to publication), many non-Classicists conflate the injured feet and the exposure, mistakenly concluding that Oedipus was put out to die *because of* this malformation. This link is not suggested in any of the Greek literature, and I believe that it is so easily accepted because of the automatic tendency to associate infanticide with deformity.[1]

Because it is often assumed that disabled babies were unwanted babies, the issue of exposure is intimately connected to the question of physical disability in ancient Greece. That the Greeks, especially the Spartans and Athenians, regularly disposed of newborns with visible physical anomalies is commonly accepted in nineteenth-, twentieth-, and twenty-first century scholarship and popular culture.[2] This assumption is so taken for granted that it is rarely backed up with documentation. It is often stated as a matter-of-fact characteristic of ancient Sparta; for example, an electronic guide to Sparta, "Where Helen and Alexander Stopped," asks, "Settling down in the town

29

square to sip ouzo and enjoy the view, who would guess that the foothills to the west are where the ancient Spartans left their weaker infants to die?"[3]

As part of the scholarly mythology, accounts of exposure in the Greek world become diluted, exaggerated, and lurid; for example, this is from a 1984 text on neonatal care:

> Young children, weak children, female children, and especially children regarded as being defective were regularly strangled, drowned, buried in dunghills, "potted" in jars to starve to death, or exposed to the elements (with the belief that the gods had the responsibility of saving exposed infants). Concerned that defective infants would, once grown, pass on their defects to the next generation, the Greeks actively promoted the destruction of anomalous infants.[4]

Yet modern literature on exposure in ancient Greece offers surprisingly little in-depth analysis of this custom of killing newborns with visible physical variations.[5] One of the more detailed treatments of the subject of exposure is Cynthia Patterson's discussion of physically anomalous newborns within the larger context of the criteria behind the decisions made in rearing or not rearing various infants. Patterson concludes that the decision to rear or dispose of a deformed infant involved many factors and could be based on considerations other than the infant's physical appearance alone.[6] Robert Garland also discusses exposure of deformed infants in the Greek world, concluding that not all deformed infants would have been destroyed.[7] Garland points out that the recommendations of the fourth-century B.C. philosophers Plato and Aristotle to destroy all deformed babies suggest the existence of the opposite practice.[8] Marc Huys, in a 1996 essay, traces the testimony for the Spartan practice of selective exposure and places the practice in a philosophical tradition of the utopian state.[9]

Ruth Oldenziel raises methodological concerns about the current studies of female infanticide, which are also applicable to a study of the infanticide of deformed infants. Oldenziel observes that in the case of female infanticide, the central questions of the realities of women's existence are obscured by modern concerns such as morality and, most recently, birth control.[10] Indeed, if an investigation of the fate of deformed infants is couched in modern terms, the larger realities, such as the cultural context of deformity, will be lost.

In this chapter, I build on the brief discussions of Patterson and Garland and expand on Huys's discussion while paying attention to the methodological concerns raised by Oldenziel. Recent work in disability studies, in the study of concepts of normalcy, and in the issue of eugenics invites a reexamination of the assumption that all or most deformed babies were destroyed. Overall, I find that too often, anachronistic assumptions about modern standards of normalcy have been applied to very thin evidence and have resulted in sweeping conclusions. It is important to consider the larger reality—the social and psychological environment—into which deformed infants were born.[11]

This chapter begins with a review of the primary literary evidence for the destruction of deformed infants and of the vocabulary therein. Next, I summarize some modern interpretations of these passages. I then examine the assumption that deformed babies were inherently abhorrent to people in the ancient world and argue that this assumption is based on culturally constructed, modern perceptions of medical and aesthetic standards that were not current in ancient Greek communities. I do not argue that no deformed baby was ever put out to die, nor do I try from the extremely limited evidence to determine details such as frequency, change over time, or variation among socioeconomic classes, though these issues are important.[12]

A modern medical guide catalogs two hundred malformations of infants and children, most of which result from genetic syndromes.[13] The malformations with which one might be born range from barely detectable conditions such as a distinctive slant of the eye to profound, distinctive spinal-cord anomalies such as spina bifida.[14] In the modern world, 3 to 7 percent of babies are born with malformations significant enough to require medical treatment.[15]

The etiological categories were not as tidy for the Greeks. Records exist of the birth of babies with physical anomalies, but because the birth of such a baby was not primarily a medical event, the records come not only from the medical texts but also from a wide range of sources, archaeological, biographical, historical, and philosophical.[16]

The Greek source material that discusses exposure in general is scant; the primary material that discusses or alludes to the exposure of deformed infants is even more limited.[17] Five short passages, ranging from the fourth century B.C. through the second century A.D., constitute what has been taken for the source material. Two passages are from the works of Plato, and there is one each from Aristotle, Plutarch, and the second-century physician of the Roman imperial period Soranus. I will summarize the passages briefly, then discuss their implications.

In the *Republic,* a philosophical analysis of justice, Plato devises a highly regulated utopian state. This state serves, he explains, as a vehicle for his inquiry (471 c–474 b). This model community, a utopia after all, does not resemble familiar Greek patterns. In contrast to the actual Greek world, some women have roles of leadership (451–57 c); the family is abolished (457 c–461 e); and the city's inhabitants do not disagree with each other (462 a–466 d). Furthermore, the offspring of the good are reared; the offspring of inferior parents, as well as any deformed offspring from the others, are to be carried away in secret (460 c).[18]

Second, in the *Theaetetus,* a dialogue on epistemology, Plato uses the birth of a child who is unworthy of being reared as metaphor for an empty idea—"a wind-egg and a falsehood" (160 e–161 a). Playing the role of midwife, Socrates asks Theaetetus, in the role of bearer of the infant, if he would feel compelled to rear such an offspring just because it is his, and not expose it. Socrates further asks Theaetetus, who is still in the role of "mother" and bearer of the infant, if he would be willing to have the infant examined (the type of examination is not specified) and if he would be unperturbed if someone underhandedly took away the "infant," even if he were giving birth for the first time. The question is never answered, and the dialogue moves away from this topic. Only conjecture allows one to interpret the theoretical infant in question as physically deformed or mentally weak, and of course in a real-life setting, as opposed to a philosophical dialogue, one would not be able to determine an infant's mental capacity at all.

Third, Aristotle considers the ideal state and proposes several highly regulated components of human organization in the *Politics.* These regulations, within a detailed caste system, include Aristotle's recommendation for the elimination of deformed infants (1328–30 a): "As to exposing or rearing the children born, let there be a law that no deformed child shall be reared" (1335 b).

Plutarch's account of the Spartan lawgiver Lycurgus, written in the first or second century A.D., is the fourth passage possibly relating to the destruction of anomalous infants. Plutarch recognizes that "nothing can be said which is not disputed" about Lycurgus himself, who lived in what Plutarch considers the remote past (approximately the ninth century B.C.) (*Lycurgus* 1). In tracing the evolution of the Spartan state under Lycurgus, Plutarch relates the Spartan system of rearing offspring (16). The elders examined all offspring. If the baby was sturdy and strong, the father was ordered to rear it. If it was ill-born or misshapen—Plutarch does not define what either term might have meant—the elders sent it to a place called Apothetae, a ravine at the foot of Mount Taygetus. Plutarch explains the Spartan belief that a life that got off to a poor start in terms of health and strength was disadvantageous to itself and to the state and illustrates his point by stating that Spartan women bathed their newborns in wine rather than water, in order to detect epilepsy.

Finally, Soranus, in his second-century A.D. manual for the head of the household, lists a set of criteria for deciding whether or not an infant is worth rearing (*Gynecology* 2.10). The midwife is to examine the infant and, after determining its gender, consider whether or not the infant meets several criteria. These include the mother's good health during pregnancy and an appropriate length of pregnancy. The infant should have a strong cry and should be complete in all its parts. It should have unobstructed orifices; no part should be sluggish or weak; the joints should bend and stretch; the infant's size and shape should be appropriate; all parts of the body should be sensitive to touch. Conditions contrary to these indicate that the infant is not worth rearing.

With the exception of Soranus's passage, the vocabulary that describes the sort of infant to be exposed is extremely vague.[19] The *Theaetetus* includes no vocabulary that might indicate the sort of unworthy infant to be discarded. The "wind-egg and falsehood" describe an idea, not an infant. Plato's passage from the *Republic* and Aristotle's from the *Politics* use two forms of "maimed" (*pêros*). This is an extremely general term for any body that deviated in outward appearance from the standard. We can sense the huge breadth of this term when Aristotle, in *Generation of Animals,* refers to the "deformity" (*pêrôsis*) of baldness (784 a), but also refers to monstrosity as the state of being very deformed (769 b), speculating that a female is technically a deformed male (737 a). Plutarch's choice of "ill-born" is extremely imprecise and could refer to the process of birthing or one's parentage as easily as it could refer to physical configuration. "Misshapen," too, is a vague term, especially when one considers how misshapen most infants appear when they first emerge. Soranus uses relatively positive and concrete terms but leaves a wide latitude for interpretation of what constitutes, for example, "an appropriate size and shape."[20] The vagueness of the vocabulary in all the passages corresponds with the vagueness of Greek vocabulary in general that describes physical peculiarities, as discussed in chapter 1.

Of these passages, only Soranus's instructions appear to be meant for practical application. Plato's *Theaetetus* supplies little useful information about the actual practice of exposure of deformed infants. Both Plato's *Republic* and Aristotle's *Politics* describe ideal societies. While a utopia mirrors reality to some extent, it is a distorted reflection. This utopian context has not gone unnoticed. In 1959, G. van N. Viljoen pointed out that "all scholars agree that what Plato stipulates [in the *Republic*] for his eutopia [*sic*] may not be used as evidence for the practice in contemporary Athens."[21] In other words, while the underlying assumption of the passages is that exposure was a practice known to all, the regulations that Plato and Aristotle put forth do not reflect actual practice.

Plutarch's account makes claims to be historical, but he is writing about the wonders of Sparta in bygone days. The passage on exposure appears between the chapter describing Spartan marriage, in which adultery was impossible (*Lycurgus* 15), and anecdotes illustrating the fanatic self-sufficiency trained into all Spartiate boys (*Lycurgus* 17).

We know little about the application of Soranus's instructions, which were directed toward the head of the household, who would choose and instruct a midwife. The criteria for what constitutes a baby worth rearing are the clearest we have, but we do not know who applied the criteria, and Patterson points out that how carefully the criteria were applied certainly depended on how much or how little the baby was wanted.[22] As I discuss later, the degree to which any given baby was wanted was affected by the economic situation of the parents, the type of and degree of disability, the gender of the infant, and so on.

It is dangerous to make too much of the scant information about exposure of any baby, deformed or not.[23] The conclusions drawn from these five passages that allude to deformed infants must be even more tentative. Even so, wide-ranging conclusions have been drawn from this limited information, such as the conclusion from the *Theaetetus* passage that the Greek midwife customarily disposed of even a first-born defective newborn, although such disposal was easier on the mother if she already had a healthy child, and the conclusion that

Soranus's passage is concrete evidence for such practice at all times in both Greek and Roman society.[24]

It has become so ingrained in popular thought that the Greeks disposed of all their deformed young that even scholars examining concepts of normalcy make categorical statements about the practice. For example, some scholars have proposed that the Greeks disposed of their deaf babies.[25] It is very difficult, though, to determine deafness in infancy. Today, only sophisticated equipment and methods of testing can determine deafness in infants; without this testing, "a permanent congenital hearing loss may escape detection for months or even years."[26] While the symptoms of deafness might be apparent within a few months, people in the ancient world would have had no way to determine the degree of the deafness, nor would they have known whether the deafness was temporary, such as hearing loss brought on by an ear infection, or permanent.[27]

Some scholars have also assumed motivations for the disposal of deformed infants. These motivations include the medical and economic burden such offspring would have caused society if they were allowed to live and the divine displeasure that a deformed baby represented.[28] The conclusions and motivations mentioned here are based on anachronistic assumptions, but they are presented in the context of a larger discussion of Greek society and are tempered by acknowledgments of the dearth of evidence.[29] Still, such conclusions are flawed, I argue following, because they are rooted in an inaccurate view of assumptions about social context. An examination of the concept of normalcy is key to understanding the cultural context into which a deformed baby was born.

The thin evidence available does not allow a conclusion about any one standard fate of infants born with visible physical anomalies. It is possible, though, to reconstruct partially the cultural atmosphere into which a defective child was born. A malformed child as a biological entity does not evoke any one certain response from the parents; rather, the birth and the response to the birth take place in their cultural context.[30] Physically deformed infants are not in themselves abhorrent.[31] There is no evidence in the Greek material that they were thought to evoke or result from divine displeasure. It is only within the larger social structure that certain groups become identified as desirable or undesirable.[32]

To consider the cultural atmosphere into which a malformed baby was born, it is necessary to examine ancient Greek attitudes toward people with visible physical disabilities. While attitudinal subtleties are impossible to reconstruct, a rough outline of the aesthetic, economic, religious, and civic consequences can be determined. While this outline cannot result in hard conclusions, it provides a counterweight to the exaggerated nineteenth-, twentieth-, and twenty-first century ideology of universal exposure of malformed infants.

As for the aesthetic consequences of deformity, the differences between the ancient and modern setting must be considered. In the developed world, one expects to deliver a baby who conforms to somatic ideals. To ensure that it will not be born otherwise, precautions—often taken—such as the amniocentesis fluid test are standard. In the ancient world, one would not have been shocked to deliver a baby with some anomaly or other.[33] Childbirth was not a medical occasion, abnormal babies were not pathologized, and in fact the health and illness of infants and children were not of medical interest.[34] A deformed baby was not necessarily seen as inferior, unattractive, or in need of medical care: these assumptions are formed by modern medical and cultural values.[35] There were standards of normalcy in the ancient world—if there were not, there would have been no category of the physically monstrous.[36] The standards, however, were indeterminate and context bound. Defined standards of normalcy for the human body arise only in modern times and are linked with the development of statistics in the nineteenth century and of eugenics in the twentieth century.[37] In other words, the stringent measurements that we use today to determine what constitutes deformity in an infant did not exist in the ancient world, and what we would call a deformed baby today would not necessarily have been an unacceptable baby in ancient Greece.

This is not to suggest that the ancient world held no concept of beauty on the one hand or ugliness on the other. Indeed, the exquisite is epitomized by Greek statuary, and the grotesque is a necessary counterpoint.[38] The Homeric tale of Aphrodite's rejection of Hephaestus on grounds of his grotesque body is a literary reflection of this aesthetic opposition (*Odyssey* 8.308–12):

> Aphrodite, daughter of Zeus, scorns me for that I am lame and loves destructive Ares because he is comely and strong of limb, whereas I was born misshapen.[39]

Athena, too, is disgusted by Hephaestus, and runs from his clumsy, amorous pursuit (Apollodorus 3.14.6).

The idea of attainable perfection, though—that a mortal can shape himself to the mathematical perfection of Greek statuary—is modern.[40] It is important to avoid projecting present-day interpretations of Classical statuary onto fifth-century Greeks. Mathematical measurements of conformation to an ideal were not applied, as they are to a fanatical degree in our own day, to the ordinary, living human body. In 1958, Robert P. Charles argued that the Greek artists modeled the human form purely on mathematical canons, producing images that did not resemble their own ethnic type.[41] In the sixth century, Hephaestus's lameness is emphasized in vase painting, as figure 2 shows; yet even though he is still known as lame throughout the Classical period, his lameness is no longer detectable in artistic depiction in the fifth century.[42]

Given the Greek philosophical ideal of symmetry and balance, it is not surprising that physical deformity usually resulted in negative aesthetic evaluation. Still, the aesthetic consequences of physical impairment were relative to the context. Recognizing an individual's physical impairment as ugly, funny, or both is quite different from the institutionalized horror of physical impairment that is reflected in the media today.[43] While we may focus on Hephaestus's failed sexual conquests, it is worth noting that there were successes as well: the god married Charis ("Grace") (Homer *Iliad* 18.382; Pausanias 9.35.1) and Aglaea, the youngest of the Graces (Hesiod *Theogony* 945), and produced a son with Anticlia (Apollodorus 3.16.1).

At any rate, a baby would not have been killed on grounds of ugliness. Destroying babies on aesthetic grounds alone was a concept so alien to Greek culture that in the first century B.C., Diodorus could entertain his audience—and possibly make a dig at the measures proposed in the *Republic*—with the tale of the utopian island encountered in the journeys of Iambulus.[44] On this island, everyone is long-lived (living up to 150 years) and healthy, and people who become sick or crippled are required by law to commit suicide (2.57.4–5). Diodorus also tells of the Indian cities ruled by King Sopeithes, encountered by Alexander the Great (17.91.4–7). India was, in the perception of most Greeks, tremendously far away and fabulously non-Greek. These Indians, Diodorus reports, putting value on beauty more than anything, destroy those who are bodily deficient as not worth bringing up.[45]

Diodorus's tales are a counterpoint to the assumption of exposure of deformed infants on aesthetic grounds. Another counterpoint is the demographic landscape of Greece discussed in chapter 1. Even if most deformed babies were killed, people with many physical anomalies would still have populated the ancient world. A recent excavation of a fifth-century burial site, for example, revealed that over 40 percent of the individuals had some bone pathology.[46]

In any case, with the exception of obvious physical variations such as missing limbs, it was difficult to judge whether a baby would retain its physical appearance or whether the child would grow out of it. All babies are weak and, of course, are unable to walk.[47] In fact, children as a group may have been seen as defective people.[48] Still, babies were not medically categorized and pathologized as they are today.

Hope of correction for even the most severe deformity did not have to be ruled out; after all, we have testimony of miraculous healings of everything from lameness to missing eyeballs.[49] Two conflicting views on how to handle babies illustrate the perceptions both that infants were prone to physical impairment and that physical impairment could be reversed. Plato would have children carried around until the age of three to prevent distortion of limbs from too much pressure (*Laws* 788 d–789 e) and admiringly reports the Persian practice of molding the limbs of their young sons to the correct shape (*Alcibiades* 1.121 e). This is echoed by Plutarch, who argues that it is necessary to mold the limbs of children so that they grow up straight, not twisted (*Moralia* 3.5 e). Interestingly, a Hippocratic author compares bandaging a fracture to swaddling an infant, as if the infant is born broken and must be mended (*On Fractures* 22).[50] Aristotle suggests that children should be subjected to as many movements as possible to prevent distortion owing to the softness of their bones (*Politics* 1336 a). One Hippocratic writer outlines the cure for clubfoot by simple manipulation and bandaging (*On Joints* 62).[51] Another Hippocratic warning—that if the dislocated limb of an infant is neglected, the whole leg will become useless and atrophied—also suggests that at least some babies with impaired limbs were treated, not destroyed (*On Joints* 55). Finally, Aristotle's injunction against rearing deformed children suggests that in ordinary conditions at least some parents did keep their deformed offspring—enough parents, at least, to warrant this scolding.[52] A possible reference to families keeping congenitally malformed babies is seen in Plutarch, where he relates the insistence of men on fathering their own babies, even if, because of their own constitutions, chances are good that the baby will be born "foolish, untimely, or diseased" (*Lycurgus* 15.8–9).

So whether by accident or decision, some babies with congenital anomalies survived. Symptoms such as juvenile rheumatoid arthritis, for example, do not manifest at birth. Furthermore, physical conditions such as limb loss, blindness, and a host of other disabilities can be acquired at any time. As discussed in chapter 1, the physical appearance of the actual population of any Greek community differed dramatically from the persistent Neoclassical image of a Greece populated by mathematically perfect human bodies and from any given developed community in the modern world. In considering the larger reality into which deformed babies were born, the physical composition of the population is not only an aesthetic factor but an economic one as well, as I discuss next. William L. Langer, in a historical survey of infanticide, writes that "infanticide has from time immemorial been the accepted procedure for disposing not only of deformed or sickly infants, but of all such newborns as might strain the resources."[53] Langer is not alone in his assumption that a deformed infant would grow up to be an economic burden. Indeed, one's economic role in the community—one's contribution to society—is very important in determining acceptance and integration into the community.[54] But this economic model equating physical deformity with economic dependence is a modern abstraction.[55] There is no intrinsic reason why a person with even a significant physical disability cannot play a productive economic role.[56]

A physical impairment *in itself* did not constitute economic dependence.[57] A physically handicapped person earning a living would not have been a remarkable sight. Because of this, the phenomenon appears in the surviving material infrequently and incidentally. We usually learn about people's physical handicaps not because they were remarkable in themselves but because permanent physical characteristics were personal, individual attributes that among other things established a person's identity. In mythology, we see the grand revelation of Odysseus's scarred foot (Homer *Odyssey* 21.221). Odysseus's limp was, earlier in the tale, a reverse identification—that is, a disguise (Homer *Odyssey* 17.203, 336–38). Perhaps the most dramatic revelation is that of Oedipus's pierced ankles, in Sophocles' *Oedipus the King* (1034). Maybe in mockery of these dramatic moments, Aristophanes uses a series of physical clues such as blindness and lameness that leads to

Telephus's identity (*Acharnians* 418–29). Indeed, a permanent physical handicap was an efficient means of identification. A private letter from the fourth century A.D., for example, identifies a certain Isaac as "the mutilated one" (*P. Oxy.* 46.3314.23).[58] Several other papyri show physical handicaps as efficient identification. A real-estate transaction from 101 B.C. identifies the owner of a house by the scar on his cheek and the limp in his right foot (*Sel. Pap.* 1.29). A tax roll from the second century A.D. shows receipts from a man who was identified as lame (*P. Mich.* 4.1.223), and a document from A.D. 211 records payment to a village official who is also identified as lame (*P. Oxy.* 19.2240.2.32).

In fact, we see people with physical handicaps involved in a wide range of economic activities. Alciphron, a second- or third-century A.D. writer, depicts a tailor who limped (*Letters of Farmers* 24.1.) A fragment of Aristophanes' comedy may refer to a lame peddler ("Anagyrus" frag. 57 *PCG*), and we learn that a first-century A.D. contract for a division of property includes a lame slave.[59] A Hippocratic author mentions that people who have congenitally withered arms, though unable to raise their elbows, can still use tools such as saws, picks, or spades (*On Joints* 12). Metalworkers and miners were especially vulnerable to injury and, having acquired a physical impairment, would have had no reason to stop working or change trades if they were capable of carrying on their trade.[60] The connection between artisans and physical impairment is reflected in Amazon lore. A Hippocratic writer relates the tale that the Amazons dislocated their sons' joints at the hip and knee and used the boys as artisans in leather and copper (*On Joints* 53). The connection between artisans and physical impairment is even more clearly reflected in the mythological figure of the divine smith Hephaestus, the crook-foot god.[61] The god is often depicted in painting with his smithing tools; even in the whimsical portrayal—a red-figure painting from the fifth-century B.C.—of drunk Hephaestus being led home by a satyr, he carries his identifying emblems, a pincers and hammer (see fig. 3).[62]

We do not know if such people began their trade as physically disabled people, or stayed in their trades after they had acquired a disability, or both. The toxicity produced by smelting metals can produce lameness; in fact, Kurt Aterman suggests that some depictions of Hephaestus may portray arsenical neuritis.[63] It is also possible that such trades were feasible and open to workers with disabilities. The point remains the same in any case: people with physical variations were not

Hephaestus is closely identified with metalworking. Here, he is carrying his smithing tools, even though he is clearly too drunk to use them. Hephaestus, drunk and supported by a satyr. Red-figure pelike, 435–430 B.C. Munich Archaeological Collection. Erich Lessing/Art Resource, N.Y.

automatically thought to be economically ineffectual, and it was within this cultural context that the decision was made about keeping or disposing of a baby with physical variations.

Religious factors certainly played a role in conditioning the social attitude to disability and thus are important to consider in attempting to reconstruct the atmosphere into which a deformed baby was born. Of course, all of these categories—aesthetic, economic, religious, and civic—are very much intertwined. The accounts of Hephaestus tell us that even a god cannot always overcome the aesthetic liability of lameness, yet they also tell us that his disability did not prevent—and in fact may have enhanced—his economic worth.

The birth of a baby with clubfoot, for example, would not necessarily have been interpreted as an economic horror, if Hephaestus is any indication, but it is reasonable to think that clubfoot, or any deformity, would have been considered a blemish. It is possible that such blemishes had religious implications. Plato, in the *Laws*, written many years after his *Republic*, is again devising the perfect community. He writes that priests should be selected by lot but that only those who are from good families and who are sound (*holoklêron*) should be eligible (759 c). Plato's rule that priests must be sound in body probably had a basis in ancient reality.[64] An Asclepiadic inscription from about 200 B.C., from Chalcedon (a Greek colony on the Bosporus), stipulates that a priest must be sound (*holoklaros*) (*SIG* 1009), and a fragment of Attic comedy refers to a law requiring priests to be sound (*holoklêrous*) (Anaxandrides 39.10–11).[65] "Sound" (*holoklêros*) has a range of meanings, from "complete" to "uncastrated," the latter term distinguishing Greek sensibilities from Eastern cults, some of which involved eunuchs.[66] Aeschines sheds light on the qualifications for priesthood in a courtroom speech, "Against Timarchus," in which he compares the moral impurity of Timarchus with that of any given candidate for priesthood who is not "pure in body" (*katharos to sôma*), according to the laws (188).[67] If one takes the meanings of the physical characteristics that would bar a man from priesthood to refer to physical disabilities as we define them, the interpretations must have been as wide open in the ancient world as they are now for the ADA. Isocrates, in the discourse "To Nicocles," implies that the priesthood is open to "any man" (*pantos andros*) (6); Demosthenes, in a prelude to a lost speech, scolds the Athenians, implying that there are no standards for their priests (*Exordia* 55.2).

Of course, an infant would not have been discarded simply because of his potential ineligibility for the priesthood. My point is that religious restrictions against people with deformities could justify and reflect an attitude that people with deformities were inferior. In the absence of conclusive evidence, though, it is impossible to say how the law against a blemished priest was put into effect or what constituted a blemish. Isocrates and Demosthenes imply that the evaluation was made "case by case" rather than by any codified set of restrictions.

The phenomenon of scapegoating—finding an outside focus for tension and anxiety—is intertwined with a religiously justified repugnance for people with certain characteristics. Greek literature gives us examples of the mockery of people with physical deformities, Thersites being the earliest and most obvious example. In the *Iliad,* the soldier Thersites is mocked and abused for his ugly appearance; indeed, his physical appearance marks him as the reverse of the Homeric hero. The treatment that Thersites receives can certainly be classified as scapegoating.[68] Scapegoat rituals, which culminated in getting rid of the scapegoat by banishment or death, were performed on "criminals, slaves, ugly persons, strangers, young men and women, and a king," all of whom, Jan Bremmer argues, are characterized by their marginal status in Greek society.[69]

In stark contrast to today's etiquette, interesting physical characteristics were noted and sometimes laughed at.[70] In comedy, we see ordinary people identified by a variety of permanent physical characteristics, including physical handicaps; for example, the fifth-century Eupolis, in "Golden Race," a comedy surviving in fragmentary form, identifies spectators as blind, hunchbacked, red-headed, and so on (frag. 298 *PCG*). That people's unusual or undesirable physical traits were pointed out, however, does not necessarily indicate that disabled people were routinely the community scapegoats or that scapegoats were routinely people with physical disabilities.

Finally, in considering the cultural atmosphere into which a deformed baby was born, the civic consequences of disability should be addressed. Two separate spheres, one for men and one for women, will be considered.

The ultimate measure of a Greek man's worth and status in his community was his capacity to participate in the military, and we see that men with a variety of physical impairments participated in some military activities. Thersites, whatever the case regarding his role as scapegoat, was not excluded from the army for being bandy-legged, lame, and humpbacked (Homer *Iliad* 2.216–219).[71] Plutarch tells the tale of a limping Spartan who explains that a limp does not prevent participation in battle: one needs to hold his ground in battle, he says, not run away (*Moralia* 234 e). Plutarch was fond of this story and seemingly repeats it at every chance he gets. In another version, a lame Spartan soldier is limping off to war, inquiring after a horse. Ironically, the lame Spartan king Agesilaus sees him and tells him that the army has need of those who stand and fight, not those who run away (*Moralia* 210 f). Closely following this tale, we read of a certain Androcleidas, who has a crippled leg and is being questioned about his military competence. He replies that he does not have to run away, but rather to stand and fight (*Moralia* 217 c). And in yet another version, a lame Spartan is limping off to war, but no one is laughing this time: he is accompanied by his mother. She admonishes him, laconically, to remember his valor with every step (*Moralia* 241 e). This version is repeated when Alexander the Great's father, Philip II, injured in the thigh and troubled by his lameness, is urged by Alexander to go forth and to remember his valor with every step (*Moralia* 331 b).

These anecdotes may tell us more about Plutarch's view of Spartan and Macedonian valor in bygone days than they do about the real experience of lame soldiers. Nevertheless, we can see, in broad outline, that one could both limp and take an active part on the battlefield.[72] Famous generals include, for example, Philip II himself, who was, by Demosthenes' account, quite lame (*On the Crown* 67).[73] In addition, Alexander the Great's leg was "shattered beneath his knee," according to Plutarch, though we are not told if the injury led to permanent disability (*Alexander* 45).

It seems that one had to be quite severely mutilated not to fight. When the otherwise unknown Aristogeiton wanted to get out of military service, Plutarch tells us, he appeared with both legs bandaged, using a staff (*Phocion* 10.1–2). Also, it is interesting that in Diodorus's account of the Amazons, the women had to maim not just one but all four limbs of the male offspring to incapacitate them for the demands of war (2.45.1–3). Men who could not walk at all may have played a military role, if not on the front lines. Plutarch describes Artemon, who designed siege engines (*Pericles* 27.3–4). Artemon was lame—apparently very lame: he had to be carried to all of his projects.[74] These accounts of disabled men's participation in the military are mythological, legendary, or anecdotal. Still, so many men of military age were physically incapable of active fighting in the field that, as Barry Baldwin suggests, there may have been an official class of men at Athens designated for garrison duty.[75]

The civic ramifications of physical impairments in women must be explored separately from those of men. Ancient Greek society had strikingly separate male and female spheres. On a general level, simply being female was considered physically disabling. Aristotle speculates that women were really deformed (*pepêrômenón*) males (*Generation of Animals* 737 a). A society's notion of the physiological body reflects the configurations of its social and political body, and it is common knowledge that in Greece, women as a class were banned a priori from fulfilling the tasks of citizenship solely because they were women.[76] No woman was a true citizen; her civic worth consisted of her potential to bear future citizens.[77] Still, women had socially prescribed roles that were part of the larger community, and these roles must be considered to speculate about how a female with a physical impairment would have been perceived. Two passages from Herodotus provide us with the bulk of the information about women with physical disabilities, as we in the present day would define disability.

The tale of Labda is set in seventh-century B.C. Corinth (Herodotus 5.92). Labda was the lame daughter of a Corinthian man of the ruling family, the Bacchiadae. Because she was lame, none of the Bacchiadae would marry her.[78] She was married into a rival clan instead and bore and raised Cypselus, who would overthrow the Bacchiadae and take rule of Corinth himself. In another tale, Herodotus admiringly reports the Babylonian system for marrying off all the females (1.196). Each year, in every village, all the females of marriageable age were gathered in one place to be auctioned off, "with a crowd of men standing around them." The auction began with the fairest of all. Eventually the commoners, who, Herodotus assures us, "cared nothing for beauty," took the misshapen and deformed ones, who were provided dowries by the revenues from the pretty women.

Herodotus's account of Labda the Lame and the account of the Babylonian marriage market constitute the bulk of the literary record of women with physical impairments. These passages illustrate two points. First, physical characteristics such as withered or missing limbs were perceived as unsightly in a female, but not disabling. Second, such physical traits did not necessarily prevent a woman from fulfilling her most important socially prescribed role, which was to bear children.

Two small tales from Herodotus make meager data. Nevertheless, these passages are what we have available. The two tales do not provide a firm basis for conclusive statements about women and physical impairment. Still, the passages illustrate the differences between the modern construction of disability and the ancient situation, in which the concept of ability and disability shifted according to individual circumstances. Furthermore, only the aristocratic social layer is revealed in these tales, while the bulk of the Greek population was nonaristocratic and rural. One can speculate, though, that the wife of a Greek peasant would have been expected to take part in farming activities.[79] This is not to suggest that only peasant women worked hard; all but the wives of the wealthiest Greek men worked in and out of the home.[80] In communities that do not waste human resources, tasks can be allocated according to individual ability. As we have seen, men who were unable to serve on the front lines of battle were able to perform garrison duty. Physical characteristics such as a missing leg or a sight impairment do not necessarily prohibit one from carrying out everyday tasks. Women who were unable to perform heavy tasks would have been able to perform less physically demanding tasks. Weeding, for example, requires less mobility than threshing.[81]

The focus of the story of Labda is certainly not on her lameness, which merely serves as an explanation for her marriage outside the clan. Indeed, the focus of the story is not even on Labda herself, but on her role as a vehicle for the transition of power in Corinth.[82] The important points for this discussion are, first, that Labda's lameness devalued her aesthetically, to the point that the Bacchiadae rejected her; and second, that the aesthetic devaluation of her limp was not thought to interfere with abilities required for the female role of successful childbearer and child rearer.

The same two points—that a physical characteristic such as lameness was an aesthetic matter but that it was not necessarily a physical disability—are inherent in Herodotus's tale of the Babylonian marriage market. Although Herodotus presents this purported system as both defunct and Babylonian, his Greek audience had to assume two points for the story to make sense. First, a deformity devalued a bride, in this case quite literally. Second, physical deformity would not in itself render a woman unable to perform her primary tasks. Physical flaws were important considerations only for those who could afford to consider aesthetics. Herodotus compares malformed women to pretty women, not to nondisabled women. The specifics of what constituted an undesirable physical deformity are lost to us, as are the specific images that Herodotus meant to convey of the malformed and deformed women—and pretty women, for that matter—in the marriage market. We do not know the range of severity of Labda's lameness that would have been pictured by the audience hearing the tale.

In any case, Herodotus's Greek audience knew that in Greece, one married the person one was contracted to marry.[83] Plato writes that marrying someone with diseases or deformities of the body or mind can make life unbearable, which suggests that such marriages were not unheard of (*Laws* 11.925e).

The most important task for a Greek woman was childbearing, and it was sterility, not deformity, that had serious and codified implications.[84] Jean-Nicolas Corvisier, in a 1985 study, found that 10 percent of women in ancient Greece were sterile or perceived to be sterile.[85] Alongside Asclepiadic testimony for recovery from blindness and paralysis and lice, we read the testimony of women who came to the temple "for offspring" and were granted their desire.[86]

Sterility would always have prohibited a woman from fulfilling her community role. Barrenness would have constituted a significant economic liability in the case of Greek women of childbearing age. In a female infant, a missing limb or an asymmetrical body, while it had aesthetic implications, did not take away the potential to fulfill what in the ancient world was the primary female task in the community. Furthermore, undesirable aesthetic characteristics could always be outgrown.

Having considered some aesthetic, economic, religious, and civic factors of deformity, the picture that emerges of the cultural atmosphere in Greece is one in which physical deformity did not necessarily evoke a negative visceral reaction, an assumption of ill health, religious horror, or the expectation of economic dependence. A physically deformed infant, then, would not necessarily have been unwelcome on these grounds.

While there is nothing to suggest absolutely that a deformed baby would have been killed solely on grounds of abnormality, there were practical considerations of the physical care of a newborn with special needs. We have no Greek descriptions of the care involved for an infant with additional needs, but a modern autobiography describes the care involved for an infant with cerebral palsy, a condition that surely existed in the ancient world, as it results from a diminished supply of oxygen at birth. Earl R. Carlson relates that, as a newborn, he was at first unable to nurse because of the spasms associated with his cerebral palsy and had to take milk from a medicine dropper. At six months, he could not sit up; he did not crawl until he was two years old.[87] It would have been possible to raise such a baby in ancient Greece—after all, feeding bottles and potty chairs did exist—but the investment of time would have been substantial.[88] In such cases, on one hand, perhaps passive infanticide was practiced; that is, the infant would not have been killed outright, but would not have received the intense attention necessary for survival.[89] On the other hand, a family in ancient Greece with the economic means may have been willing and able to invest the time and care necessary to raise such a child, perhaps especially if it were a firstborn male.[90]

In summary, the source material that discusses deformed offspring in the ancient Greek world is too thin to conclude that their destruction was standard practice. The cultural atmosphere into which such babies were born was one in which deformed people were not categorically deemed evil, worthless, or ill. Modern assumptions about the economic worth and aesthetic appeal of deformed people, cloaked in the standards of medical health, do not provide an appropriate framework of interpretation for the evidence about the lot of anomalous infants in ancient Greece.

The choice of rearing or not rearing a deformed baby would have rested on factors of convenience or, especially in the case of a female, aesthetics, but not on factors of disability as we in the modern, developed world understand disability. It was later in Western thought—Lennard Davis proposes the eighteenth century as the point of transition—that people with physical handicaps became a distinct category, the objects of pity and fear, deserving of charity and scorn.[91] This attitude toward disabled people as a group is not apparent in the Greek sources. This is not to say that the Greeks were particularly enlightened or humanitarian. Deformed people such as Hephaestus and Thersites were mocked and scapegoated, and while both are literary characters, surely the attitude reflects real life to some extent. That some Greeks made fun of some disabled people, though, does not prove that all Greeks killed all their deformed offspring.

Why, then, is it so embedded in popular culture that the Greeks disposed of their malformed infants? Marc Huys concludes that both Greek and modern utopianists suggest that a condition of the perfect society is "to nip its non-perfect members in the bud."[92] In our mythology, we describe the ancient Greek practice of infanticide in such extreme terms in order to justify our discomfort with disability and our culture's desire to rid the world of people with disabilities. In painting a society of Greeks who routinely disposed of their deformed infants, we are holding our own, advanced society—in which there are two distinct groups, able (us) and disabled (them)—up for comparison: we label them kindly, we treat them as "almost normal," and we do not stare. We treat disabled people better than the Greeks did because we treat them with compassion: we can cure them, rehabilitate them, make them "normal." If we determine that they do not have the potential to be a Helen Keller or a Stevie Wonder, we can ensure that they're not even born. In addition, perhaps there is some wistful retrospect in the Greek utopian scenario as well: in a simpler time, in the absence of medical technology and medical ethics, there were no difficult decisions to make. Today, the decisions can be agonizing: "In a moment in U.S. history when medical technologies and social policies have combined to make it fashionable neither to have a child with disabilities nor to hide such children away in institutions, mothers are left to take the full brunt of responsibility and blame."[93]

The popular depiction of exposure in Athens and Sparta says more about present-day beliefs about our present-day society than it does about ancient Greek communities. The following chapter continues to highlight the dangers of anachronistic assumptions.

3 Demosthenes' Stutter ∾

Demosthenes, the fourth-century Athenian orator, is today both an emblem of rhetorical skill and a model of overcoming disability. The story that is told about Demosthenes overcoming his physical impairment feeds into the stereotype that disability is a personal hardship that can, and should, be overcome.

It is commonly reported that Demosthenes overcame a speech impairment by various exercises such as holding pebbles in his mouth while speaking. An on-line encyclopedia, for example, says that, affected with a speech impediment, "he resorted to unusual means to overcome his defect."[1] Almost any text on speech pathology, if its author provides a historical overview, includes mention of Demosthenes.[2] A resource center for stutterers in the Netherlands takes the name "Demosthenes."[3]

We do not actually know what sort of speech disorder Demosthenes had or indeed if he had any at all.[4] In fact, we have little information about any individual in the ancient world with a speech disorder. Still, it is possible to discuss the cultural context of speech disorders in general in the Classical Greek world. The population of the ancient Greek world included people with what would be called, in English, speech disorders, but oddities of speech were seen as personal characteristics, not as pathology. Since there was no concept of speech pathology, we have no coherent medical record.

The limited amount of material we do have about speech disorders in ancient Greece comes by way of many different authors in a variety of genres over the span of about a thousand years. Still, the presence of speech disorders in the Greek world can be conjectured from the etiology of terms having to do with speech, the subject of the first section of this chapter. Next, I take up the ancient scientific and medical record, followed by a discussion of some broad attitudes about speech disorders in the ancient world that can be determined by looking at the Greek vocabulary. Then, I compare the records of Alcibiades and Demosthenes. Alcibiades, a fifth-century politician and philanderer, was well known for his lisp. Far from overcoming his lisp by hard work, Alcibiades seems to have made the most of it, using it to enhance his charm. Ancient attitudes toward speech impairment, including the perceived speech impairment of women, are summarized in light of the background of Alcibiades and Demosthenes. In the final section of the chapter, I compare the legacy of these two figures in terms of contemporary disability-rights issues.

The speech disorders that one can safely assume to have affected people in the ancient world as in the present day include stuttering, anatomically caused disorders, developmental disorders, and impairments associated with old age. I discuss each briefly following.

While the cause of stuttering is unknown, it has a biological basis that is likely neurological and is found throughout all cultures and languages today; that is, it is not related to culture or language.[5] About 1 percent of the population in the United States stutters, and there is no reason to think that this figure would have been markedly different in the ancient world or in any society since language developed.[6]

Other speech disorders have anatomical causes that were present in ancient Greeks. In any historical period, the structure of the face and mouth determines one's ability or inability to articulate sounds fluently.[7] Although babies in Greece born with cleft palates or other conditions that prevented them from suckling would not have survived, those born with less significant cleft palates who did survive would not have had the benefit of corrective surgery, a routine matter in the modern, developed world.[8] Other kinds of damage to the structure of the face and mouth could also have been acquired later in life, for example, from accident. Malocclusion, the faulty meeting of the upper and lower teeth, was also common. We know from skeletal evidence that dental problems were common, some of which must have affected speech.[9]

A developmental speech disorder, in contrast to the anatomical disorder discussed earlier, refers to patterns of pronunciation and the process of learning to talk.[10] Of present-day children with speech disorders, only half achieve speech fluency without special training.[11] So, in the presumed absence of formal speech therapy in the ancient world, it is likely that at least half of the children with speech disorders did not grow out of their speech disorders. Also, children whose speech disorder results from motor problems associated with cerebral palsy, muscular dystrophy, or spina bifida do not progress to fluent speech in the modern world and likewise would not have achieved fluent speech in the ancient world.[12]

In addition to congenital and developmental causes, speech disorders of all sorts can be acquired at any point in life, for example, as a result of head injury, including cerebrovascular accident ("stroke").[13] Stuttering is a possible result of a blow to the head.[14] Furthermore, speech disorders can be acquired from the complications associated with aging.[15]

So we have indications that a wide variety of speech disorders were present in the ancient Greek world. But how did the ancient Greeks themselves think of speech disorders? There was no concept of speech pathology among the Greeks, though some scientific and medical authors did take an interest in speech disfluencies as physiological phenomena.

The Hippocratic writers were the first to recognize classes of people who had various difficulties with speaking. Mentioned rarely, the conditions are not treated as pathologies but are considered merely as clues in diagnosing other pathologies, much as were personal characteristics such as appearance or habits of behavior. A Hippocratic writer records a winter epidemic on the island of Thasos, for example, that killed certain types of people, including black-haired people, black-eyed people, reckless drinkers, people with stumbling speech, the rough voiced, the lispers, and those quick to anger (*Epidemics* 1.2.9). Ancient writers, even the medical writers, never overtly distinguish between speech disorders and voice disorders.

Pseudo-Aristotle states that people with unclear speech are, as a whole, melancholic, as are those who lisp (*Problems* 903 b). He explains that both groups of people follow their imaginations too freely, yet their organs are too slow. This conclusion may have come, in part, from observation of facial expressions and gestures of people with articulation disorders. The slurred speech of people whose motor control of speech mechanisms has been damaged neurologically, along with the altered structure and intonation of their voice, may have been misinterpreted as resulting from mood rather than physiology.[16]

Greek understanding of the physiology of speech disorders focuses on the tongue. Pseudo-Aristotle, for example, writes that the tongue does not obey the speaker's intention (*Problems* 902 b). He also suggests that faltering speech results from a chilling of the parts used to speak and adds his observation that people with faltering speech can connect their words more easily when those parts are heated by wine (*Problems* 905 a). Aristotle posits that the tongue is loosely fastened in the case of those with faltering speech (*tois psellois*) and tightly fastened in those who lisp (*tois traulois*) (*History of Animals* 492 b).[17] Plutarch reasons that each part of the body has its own particular weakness or defect, such as blindness in the eye, lameness in the leg, and faulty speech (*psellotéta*) in the tongue (*Moralia* 963 c–d).

That the tongue governs speech makes sense intuitively. Not until the second century A.D., when Galen identified the larynx and trachea (2.589–90) and found that the tongue was governed by the brain, did the medical writers have any reason to treat the disorders themselves as pathologies (8.229).[18]

The Hippocratic terms paint a descriptive portrait of symptoms rather than define a medical condition. Still, the vocabulary used to describe speech disorders provides insight into the ancient cultural context of speech impairment. A survey of the Greek vocabulary shows that speech disorders were portrayed as a set of symptoms, not described by their causes.[19] The Greek vocabulary does not correspond closely to the modern vocabulary of speech pathology; the very concept of "speech disorder" as a discrete pathology, after all, is modern and somewhat artificial, as speech pathologists recognize.[20]

Three main Greek terms, with their standard translations, encompass speech disfluencies: *traulos* (lisp; also used to describe the twittering of a swallow); *psellos* (faltering speech); and *ischnophônos* (literally, a dry, withered, or lean [*ischnos*] voice [*phônê*]), a general term for unclear speech. These translations are generic. It is dangerous to assign more specific definitions than these, because the meaning of each term shifts from author to author and context to context. The ancient categories of speech disorders were not as exclusive as they are in the twenty-first century; for example, of lisping (*traulos*), Pseudo-Aristotle says that it is an inability to control a certain letter *and* an inability to add one syllable quickly to another, the latter of which better describes stuttering than lisping (*Problems* 902 b). A fourth term, stutter (*battos*), is rare in the Classical period.[21] None of these four terms appears before the sixth century B.C.

The terms have a wide range of meanings, many of which do not refer to the mechanical way in which words are pronounced. What Aeschylus, for example, indicates by "faltering speech" (*psellon*) is not the way in which Prometheus pronounces the words themselves; rather, "faltering" refers to the meaning of the words.

> If any of this is indistinct and difficult for you,
> Go back to it again, and clearly learn it all. (*Prometheus Bound* 816–17)[22]

The term for faltering speech (*psellos*) can refer to the meaning behind written words, as well. In the earliest example (second century B.C.) of this term's reference to the meaning behind written words, a man is cautioned to avoid expressing himself incoherently (*epipsellôs*) when he records an inventory (*P. Tebt.* 3.1.763).

The Greek vocabulary is unclear about types of speech disorders and even less clear about the degree or permanency of any given disorder. Even when a term refers to the way in which words are uttered, it never in itself indicates the degree of the speaker's disfluency. There is an enormous difference between a debilitating stutter and the stammering that anyone can have now and then, in excitement or confusion. Yet there is no distinction in the Greek vocabulary for speech disorders— and no reason that there should be—between a significant disorder and, for example, the temporarily wine-slurred utterance mentioned by the second-century A.D. writer Philostratus Major (*Imagines* 330.5).

In fact, the same vocabulary can also indicate poor pronunciation or the speech of the uneducated. A third-century A.D. runaway slave, Philippus, is identified, along with his light complexion and broad nose, by means of his "speaking badly" (*psellon*) (*P. Oxy.* 51.3616). It is tempting to take "*psellon*" as "stammer," which would make it an efficient identifying characteristic, paralleling the identifying physical characteristics discussed in the previous chapter. But identification by rough manners is common enough in other documents of this nature, so that the term should probably be taken in its general sense, "speaking badly."

Furthermore, the same term that describes adult lisping (*traulos*) (e.g., Plutarch *Alcibiades* 1) is used to describe the prattling of young children.[23] Aristophanes, in *Clouds*, has Strepsiades, who is aghast that his son has become a father beater, reprimand his son Pheidippides by implying that he had been an attentive father: "I understood your lisping" (*traulizontos*) (1381).[24] A grave stele from the second century B.C. refers lovingly to the childish lisping (*traulos*) of a dead two year old.[25] All the other three main terms as well, not only "lisping" (*traulos*), can describe childish speech. Pseudo-Aristotle asks why boys are more inclined to indistinct speech (*ischnophônos*) than men and suggests that it is because boys have less control over their bodies in general than men (*Problems* 902 b). Plutarch refers to a child mumbling (*psellizontôn*) and learning to speak (*Moralia* 496 b).

The term "stutter" (*battos*) is problematic. Battus, according to Herodotus, was the seventh-century B.C. founder of the colony Cyrene, in Africa, and the great-great-grandfather of the lame Battus (4.155–58). The name of this older Battus eventually became synonymous with stuttering, but there is actually only a vague association between Battus and speech when he is mentioned in pre-Classical and Classical writings.[26] Herodotus tells us that Battus went to the Delphic oracle to ask about his voice and received, as a typically enigmatic oracular reply, an order to found a colony (4.155).[27] Perhaps the Greeks knew how Battus's speech sounded when Herodotus described it as "unclear and lisping" (*ischophônos kai traulos*). "Unclear and lisping" does not evoke the stuttering with which Battus was later associated, but ancient Greek audiences watched and listened to tales rather than reading them. For all we know, an onomatopoeic rendition of stuttering or lisping accompanied the recitation.[28] While the name Battus and the term "stutter" (*battos*) are related, Herodotus may have had it backward (4.150). The term "stutter" is probably the older term; thus, King Battus took, rather than gave, the name for stuttering.[29]

Strabo, a historian and geographer who lived from the first century B.C. to the first century A.D., writes that "to stutter" (*battarizein*), "to lisp" (*traulizein*), and "to speak indistinctly" (*psellizein*) are onomatopoeic (*Geography* 14.2.28). Rather than clarifying any of the terms, this only opens up a wider variety of interpretations; for example, does "to speak indistinctly" (*psellizein*) correspond to our modern term "lisp" because the initial sibilant would be difficult for a person who lisps to produce? Or does the word itself sound slurred? The vocabulary is descriptive, not classificatory, and relies on context for specific meaning.

The vocabulary in the surviving material does not allow us to talk about speech pathology in general in the ancient world, but it does allow us to talk about individuals who exhibited peculiarities of speech. From there, we can continue to identify the cultural context of what we call speech disorders. Having imperfect speech—from whatever cause—was significant enough to merit some discussion in the ancient literature of the cases of Alcibiades and Demosthenes.

In the case of Alcibiades, the information is quite specific. The audience attending Aristophanes' comedy *Wasps* heard an actor replacing one liquid with another—"r" for "l"—mocking Alcibiades' characteristic manner of speech (*Wasps* 44). We do not know if the mocking was by exact imitation, by approximation, or—most likely—by exaggeration. Even if Aristophanes, Alcibiades' contemporary, provided an exact rendition, the degree of severity of Alcibiades' speech peculiarity is lost, though it must have been mild enough that he was intelligible; he was, after all, a politician, thus a rhetor. In fact, his oratorical skills are praised by none other than Demosthenes (*Against Meidias* 145).

Alcibiades' lisp seems to have been regarded as a charming peculiarity. According to Plutarch, Alcibiades' characteristic manner of speech "made his talk persuasive and full of charm" (*Alcibiades* 1.4). While the lisp (*traulos*) itself was seen as a flaw, Plutarch quips that one can forgive anything in the object of one's affections, even lisping (*traulotétas*) or pallor (*Moralia* 1 e, 84 f, 90.7 a).[30] Alcibiades' lisp was so endearing that his son, Plutarch claims, imitated it (*Alcibiades* 1.4). Alcibiades flaunted the lisp rather than trying to correct it.

We do not have descriptions of Demosthenes' voice from his contemporaries. Demosthenes seems to have had a childhood difficulty with speaking well, if not a speech disorder proper. The main source on the life of Demosthenes, Plutarch, tells us that when he was a boy, Demosthenes' speech was unpleasant to his audience (*Demosthenes* 4.5) and that as a young man he delivered his first orations with "a certain weakness of voice and indistinctness of speech and shortness of breath" (*Demosthenes* 6.3). The vagueness of this information is compounded by the five centuries between Demosthenes' life and Plutarch's biography of it.

How much fact and how much allegory was reflected is also in question. Demosthenes' bodily weaknesses were probably used as metaphors to some degree for a weak nature that allegedly led him to accept bribes from representatives of Alexander the Great (Plutarch *Demosthenes* 25). Cicero tells us that Demosthenes was a stutterer (*balbus esset*), unable even to pronounce the "r" in "rhetoric," and that he improved his declamatory style, hindered especially by shortness of breath, by declaiming verses while holding pebbles in his mouth (*On the Orator* 1.61.260–61). Plutarch, too, tells us that Demosthenes corrected his "indistinctness and lisping" by holding pebbles in his mouth while speaking and that he improved his weak voice by strengthening his lungs (*Demosthenes* 11.1). Quintilian, the first-century A.D. rhetorician, describes Demosthenes' practice of studying on the seashore to learn concentration amid the noise of the waves so that he could later concentrate amid the noise of the courtroom (10.3.30).[31]

Demosthenes does not seem to have retained any sort of difficulty with his speech as an adult. It is modern thinking that tries to associate his nickname "Batalus" (Asshole) with the Battus, discussed earlier, who is after all only tenuously connected with stuttering. Demosthenes' contemporary and rival, the orator Aeschines, says that Demosthenes had the childhood nickname Batalus because of his vulgarity, but never connects the nickname to Battus the stutterer (Aeschines *Against Timarchus* 126, 131; *On the False Embassy* 99). Demosthenes, when he acknowledges Aeschines' use of his nickname, in no way suggests that it has to do with a speech disorder. Even Plutarch, no stranger to imaginative etymologies, does not suggest that connection. Instead, he primly suggests that "Batalus" refers to "one of the parts of the body which is not decent to name" and goes on to associate Demosthenes' *other* nickname, Argas, with his manner of speech (*Demosthenes* 4.7–8). Even here, Plutarch is not sure whether Argas played on a poetic word for snake and referred to Demosthenes' rude manners or if he referred to a composer of vile songs named Argas and thus to Demosthenes' irritating style of speech.[32]

We have no direct testimony from anyone with a speech disorder in the ancient Greek world. The surviving Greek material does not allow us to determine who did and who did not have what would now be described as a speech disorder, nor does it allow insight into specific disorders. This is a natural result of looking at a phenomenon whose concept was not well defined in the ancient world. We can conclude, though, that speech disorders themselves, if not the people affected by them, were seen unfavorably. Articulate speech was needed for civic participation; it was more than just an interpersonal skill. Every man functioned as best he could in this oral civic culture. Public speaking was an important mark of civic responsibility, duty, and membership in ancient Athenian society, and the course of the Athenian community, in political, military, judicial, and religious matters, was steered by the one who had the most convincing argument. A good argument, though, had everything to do with presentation. The presentation of an argument could transcend the mechanics of rhetorical technique: the quality of the voice itself had the potential to sway one's audience. In the *Iliad*, Nestor and Odysseus are praised not just for their military cunning but for their skill in crafting and speaking words. Nestor, for example, is "the fair-spoken," "the lucid speaker of Pylos, from whose lips the streams of words ran sweeter than honey" (Homer *Iliad* 1.247–49). Odysseus's outward appearance was not promising—"you would call him a sullen man, and a fool likewise"—

> But when he let the great voice go from his chest, and the words came drifting down like the winter snows, then no other mortal man could stand up against Odysseus. (Homer *Iliad* 3.220–23)[33]

Indeed, voice quality was a significant part of a package of masculine virtues. Aristotle speaks for at least a portion of the upper classes when he describes the effective man:

> Other traits generally attributed to the great-souled man are a slow gait, a deep voice, and a deliberate utterance; to speak in shrill tones and walk fast denotes an excitable and nervous temperament. (*Nicomachean Ethics* 4.3.34)[34]

This is not to suggest that any Greek man with a less than booming voice would have been considered unmanly. Sophocles is reputed to have been unable to perform his own tragedies because his voice was weak, yet this characteristic alone did not bar him from fulfilling other masculine roles; for example, the same source—a late and anonymous biographer—narrates that he was involved in government and that he trained boys in wrestling and music.[35]

There was a wide range of attitudes toward speech disorders. At one extreme, we have the words that Plato assigned to the character Callicles, who declares that faltering speech (*psellizomenon*) is suitable and natural to a little child, but that "when one hears a grown man slurring his words . . . it strikes one as something ridiculous and unmanly, that deserves a whipping" (*Gorgias* 485 b–c). Similarly, Plutarch warns that one should not copy Plato's stoop or Aristotle's lisp (*traulismon*) lest one be contaminated with baseness (*Moralia* 26 b, 53 d). Herodotus's audience had to accept that Battus's manner of speech was troublesome enough to take him to the Delphic oracle; Demosthenes' childhood speech problems were part of a package of weaknesses that made him despicable; the attractiveness of Alcibiades' faulty speech was noted because it was a novelty.

At the other extreme, Plutarch presents speech disorders as mere cosmetic flaws. In his etiquette lesson for a host, he cautions that one should not ask a bald guest to comb his hair or a lame man to dance, nor should one order men with faltering speech (*psellois*) to sing (*Moralia* 621 e–f). The third-century A.D. biographer of philosophers, Diogenes Laertius, too, describes Aristotle's lisp (*traulos*), along with other physical characteristics such as his thin legs (*Aristotle* 5.1.1).

In short, no single set of ancient attitudes can be summarized. We see that people with speech disorders existed and functioned in society. Each case of speech impairment was a separate negotiation between the individual and his community. Women, however, at least in Classical Athens, were thought to be constitutionally incapable of entering into this negotiation. Cultural symbols of physical impairment were attributed to the female voice, thus barring women, on the basis of their very nature, from oratory. Men could overcome peculiarities of speech or use them to their advantage, but women were perceived as inherently lacking rhetorical skill. The impaired female anatomy provided a legitimizing barrier between women and oratory.

Women's speech was pathologized, not as a disorder itself but as symptomatic of the constitutional problems of being female. As discussed in the previous chapter, women in the ancient world were thought to be physically inferior to men. Female vocal cords, like the rest of their bodies, were thought to be naturally underdeveloped. Aristotle compares women's voices to those equally impotent voices of boys and eunuchs (*Problems* 903 a). On top of the chronic disability of weak vocal cords, women's bodies were perceived as simply not equipped to make them effective speakers. The marks of physical inadequacy inherent in all females were thought to affect not only voice quality but also communication faculty and capacity for reason.

Classical physiology was in part based on a balance of the humors—black and yellow bile, phlegm, and blood—that determine the body's constitution. Indeed, menstruation signified traumatic and disabling chronic ill health resulting from the imbalance of bodily fluids.[36] Women were observed to be colder, moister, and weaker than men, as a result of the chronic imbalance of these humors.[37] Women, it was thought, were literally impotent: they could not produce the white-hot semen that men produced.

Furthermore, even if a woman could develop an adequate voice, the unbalanced female body made it impossible for a woman to think rationally in the first place. From the Hippocratic perspective, the concentration of moisture, and especially blood, in the breasts and pelvic region drew blood away from the reasoning faculty and made women unreasonable, erratic, and prone to madness.[38]

The physiology of women was further complicated by the capricious nature of the uterus, which, whenever it wandered and misbehaved, made women prone to muteness, deafness, and other impairments of communication (e.g., the Hippocratic *Nature of Women* 8.3; *On Virgins* 8.466). Medical history, from the records of the Hippocratics to those of twentieth-century American physicians, often tells us that the womb is the source of irrationality in women and consequent unpredictability.

Although females, by their nature, were thought to be incapable of civic rationality, a woman's voice could serve as a channel for the supernatural.[39] The most famous example is the oracular Pythia at Delphi, whose ravings had to be interpreted by a male priest. Plutarch describes the careful balance this woman needed to attain in order to serve as a proper channel for the god:

> For many annoyances and disturbances of which she is conscious, and many more unperceived, lay hold upon her body, and filter into her soul; and whenever she is replete with these, it is better that she should not go there and surrender herself to the control of the god, when she is not completely unhampered (as if she were a musical instrument, well strung and well tuned), but in a state of emotion and instability. (*Moralia* 437 d)[40]

The Pythia was fact, but the stereotype of the dangerously unbalanced female was emphasized in myth and tragedy. Medea, mad with grief and fury at being abandoned by Jason and cut off from the civic resources of Corinth, calls on the power of Hecate, the goddess of magic and sorcery, instead:

> For, by Queen Hecate, whom above all divinities
> I venerate, my chosen accomplice, to whose presence
> My central hearth is dedicated, no one of them
> Shall hurt me and not suffer for it! Let me work:
> In bitterness and pain they shall repent this marriage,
> Repent their houses joined, repent my banishment. (Euripides *Medea*
>   394–99)[41]

In both cases, female speech, while not a civic tool, was socially dangerous nonetheless, a powerful irrational force also expressed in mythological female figures such as the Medusa, Pandora, and the Sirens.[42]

Women's speech was thought to be very different from men's speech in basic and inherent ways. Women's speech was feared as a tool within the realm of the irrational and devalued, perceived as false currency within rational discourse.[43] Whatever his problems with speaking were, with practice, Demosthenes was able to reach his natural potential of public speaking; after all, he had the underlying rational constitution. Alcibiades was able to turn his speech impediment into an ornamentation of his natural rhetorical skills. Some Greek goddesses, such as Athena, not bound to the human form of female physiology, were able to reach full human potential, that is, to be rational, intelligent, and eloquent. But it would have been useless for mortal women, permanently and by nature incapacitated, to cultivate or simulate male rhetoric.

Aspasia, the mistress of the fifth-century Athenian statesman Pericles, is at first glance an exception to the lack of participation of women in public speaking, because she was celebrated for her rhetorical skills. Aspasia is the most notorious of the *hetairai*, female prostitutes who supplied intellectual as well as sexual companionship to men. But occasional exceptions can validate, rather than invalidate, the societal norm, as is seen in the more recent phenomenon of the freak show, in which "savages" were put on display performing "civilized" activities such as reading aloud.[44] Aspasia, though skilled in rhetoric, is reported to have trained male orators, but never to have ventured into public speaking herself.[45] In any case, the historical Aspasia is lost to us. Madeleine Henry explains that when Plato illustrates the untrustworthiness of rhetoric in the *Menexenus,* the main extant source of information about Aspasia, he "supplies the words of a woman, not a man; of a foreigner, not a citizen; of a whore, not a wife; of the parent of a bastard, not a citizen; of Aspasia."[46]

Another apparent exception to the rule of women's incapacity as orators is Lysistrata, who rallies her Panhellenic female troops by the power of her argument. But Aristophanes' portrayal of Lysistrata was meant to be a hilarious absurdity: this woman (on the ancient stage, actually a male actor dressed as a woman) takes on two male attributes of which women were thought to be constitutionally incapable: weaponry and rhetoric. In his earlier *Ecclesiazusae,* too, Aristophanes sets up a hilarious premise in which women dress as men and conduct the Athenians' civic business. Aristophanes was fond of this sort of ridiculous situation, but only in comedy do dogs litigate, birds govern, or women declaim.

A speech impediment itself was not seen as a disability; rather, the constitution of a type—in this case, the female type—determined ability or inability to speak well. Women's voices could be dangerous, powerful, and prophetic, but the female voice, because it came from the female body, was impotent in the civic arena. It is no surprise to read Pericles' admonition to women who have recently become widows (Thucydides 2.45.2). This funeral oration of Pericles is the leading statesman's address to the Athenian populace at the public funeral for those killed in battle at the outset of the Peloponnesian War. After eloquently addressing the fathers, the sons, and the brothers of the dead at some length, he advises the women not to transgress "the standard which nature has set for your sex" by attracting attention in any way:

> If I am to speak also of womanly virtues, referring to those among you who will henceforth be in widowhood, I will sum up all in a brief admonition: Great is your glory if you fall not below the standard which nature has set for your sex, and great also is hers of whom there is least talk among men whether in praise or in blame. (Thucydides 2.45.2)[47]

On several levels, and with the possible occasional exception of some *hetairai,* women had no rational voice in Classical Athens. Women were not only destined by nature to be silent in public; the logical parallel is that the ideal woman was the one least mentioned. Because this principle was cloaked in etiquette, or in other words institutionalized, it is no surprise that the lives of all but the most extraordinary Athenian women are lost from the ancient historical record.[48]

The physical condition that barred people from oratory in Greece was that of being female, not necessarily that of having a speech impairment. All men had the potential to speak well, and having what we would call a speech impairment was incidental. It is Alcibiades, not Demosthenes, who has the better-documented speech impairment. We learn about Alcibiades' lisp from his contemporary Aristophanes, while Plutarch, the main source on Demosthenes' voice, never heard it—Plutarch lived five centuries later.

Yet it is Demosthenes, not Alcibiades, who is the modern emblem of speech impairment. Neither man is portrayed as a hero in the ancient sources. Alcibiades' reputation as traitor and philanderer makes him a less likely candidate for emulation, but Demosthenes was not beloved by his countrymen either.[49] Cicero's admiration for Demosthenes, along with the fact that Demosthenes is quoted far more often than any other source throughout Hermogenes' *Art of Rhetoric,* from the second century A.D., helps explain his survival as an emblem of rhetorical skills, but not as a model of overcoming disability. Perhaps Demosthenes has fared better across the centuries as a model of successful speech therapy because Alcibiades' lisp has come to be associated with the stereotype of effeminate homosexuality.[50] It is possible, too, that Alcibiades' apparent lack of desire to overcome his lisp further contributes to his lack of appearance in texts on speech pathology.

That Demosthenes was not especially associated with stuttering in the ancient world, and that he may have had nothing more than a childhood problem of mumbling, are beside the point. He has acquired the stereotypical status of historical validity, of being a "first." More important, he represents to the modern world as well as to the ancient the model of overcoming a natural defect by discipline and determination, by "diligent perseverance" (Cicero *On the Orator* 1.61.260–61). The message that overcoming a defect leads to dignity is plainly seen in various media (see fig. 4, which appeared in the November 2000 issue of *Cosmopolitan* and elsewhere).[51]

There is nothing wrong with hard work and determination, and nothing wrong with any person's wish to overcome a speech disorder or with those who offer the resources to help them do so. But the con-

Stuttering Didn't Keep Her Grounded.

Annie Glenn, wife of astronaut John Glenn,
was grounded for years by a stuttering problem.
Speech therapy and hard work turned it around.
Today she speaks with confidence,
grace, and strength.

For more information on what you can do about stuttering,
write or call us toll-free.

STUTTERING
FOUNDATION
OF AMERICA

A Nonprofit Organization
Since 1947—Helping Those Who Stutter

www.stutterSFA.org • stutter@vantek.net

1-800-992-9392

3100 Walnut Grove Road, Suite 603 • P.O. Box 11749 • Memphis, TN 38111-0749

This public service advertisement, while well meaning and probably helpful, reflects the culture from which it comes; specifically, it reflects the idea that overcoming a disability as much as possible results in dignity. The rhetoric of overcoming casts disability in the light of personal misfortune. "Stuttering Didn't Keep Her Grounded." Used with permission from the Stuttering Foundation of America, Memphis, Tenn.

cept behind valorizing those who overcome a disability is a separate issue. As Simi Linton explains in her work on disability studies, "The ideas embedded in the *overcoming* rhetoric are of personal triumph over a personal condition."[52] Disability becomes a personal misfortune rather than a political situation. Also embedded in this rhetoric of overcoming is the assumption that, if it is impossible to overcome a physical characteristic, one should at least want to overcome it. Not so long ago, if an African American acted white, he or she was a "credit to the race," lauded for doing everything possible to overcome the supposed handicaps associated with the immutable physical facts.[53] The campaigns of Christopher Reeve to find a cure for quadriplegia, the emphasis on oral education for deaf children, and the manufacture of nonfunctional and sometimes painful artificial limbs are all examples that underscore the notion that one should, at the least, be ashamed of one's physical condition if it involves a disability.[54] Being satisfied with, or even flaunting, physical disability is, in the words of the poet and activist Cheryl Marie Wade, "a sock in the eye with gnarled fist."[55]

The model of overcoming plays a role in justifying discrimination by justifying deep beliefs about disability. A commitment to making the environment equally accessible to all members of the human community necessitates a shift in outlook "from pathology to identity."[56] As long as the ideal of individual sufferers overcoming their misfortune is in place, this shift is unlikely to happen.

Demosthenes was a statesman, an orator, and an Athenian citizen, and his story is a product of his time, not our time. That Demosthenes would be known to the modern world for his rhetorical skills would no doubt have pleased him; that he would be known for stuttering would have surprised him. While not necessarily the stuff of historical truth, the story of Demosthenes' cure for speech impairment is part of the fabric of underlying and misleading beliefs about disability.

4 Croesus's Other Son ∾

In the previous chapters, I have pointed out that in the absence of medical categorizations of disability, people with disabilities were generally seen on their own terms, rather than as part of a pitiable group. If I have painted a utopian picture of ancient Greek attitudes to people with disabilities, this chapter will serve as a corrective. In the case of deafness, physiological and cultural misunderstanding led to grim circumstances for some deaf people. Deafness, as I explain in this chapter, was perceived not as a physical handicap but as an impairment of reasoning and basic intelligence.[1]

The historian Herodotus, writing in the fifth century, tells the tale of Croesus's sixth-century Lydian kingdom (Herodotus 1.34, 1.38, 1.85). Croesus, the richest man in the world, was fated to lose what he valued most: his son Atys and his Lydian kingdom. But Croesus, according to Herodotus, had two sons. Atys was noble and promising; the other son, whose name is never given, held no promise at all, for he was deaf. Despite Croesus's best efforts, Atys dies, and when Croesus fails in his plans to conquer the Persians, losing his own kingdom in the process, his fate is complete. Just as Croesus is about to die at the hands of his captors, this deaf-mute son regains his voice at the last minute in order to save his father from the pyre.

Herodotus's tale of Croesus's anonymous deaf-mute son is the only significant instance of a deaf person's appearance in the surviving

Greek literature. Other references to deafness are sparse. While the tale does not allow a reconstruction of everyday life for deaf and hearing-impaired people, it does allow an investigation into the cultural environment in which deaf people lived. Attitudinal subtleties are lost, but we can still determine broad cultural assumptions that shaped the realities of hearing-impaired people.

This chapter begins with a survey of the etiology of deafness. Next, an examination of the term "deaf" (*kôphos*) reveals both that the term was flexible in its range of meanings and that deafness was inextricably intertwined in Greek thought with the impairment in verbal communication that accompanies it. A review of the Greek medical understanding of deafness, as well as medical and nonmedical treatments for deafness, will illuminate Greek attitudes toward deaf people.

One deaf boy, who was not even Greek, is hardly representative of the portion of the ancient Greek population that was hearing impaired, as the following etiological survey suggests. Environmental and hereditary causes of deafness in the modern world also existed in the ancient world. There is no reason to doubt that a similar percentage—nearly 10 percent—of the ancient population was profoundly deaf, severely deaf, or otherwise hearing impaired. In the United States today, there are about twenty-two million hearing-impaired people; of these, two million are profoundly deaf (unable to hear anything) or severely deaf (unable to hear much).[2] Put another way, one person in a hundred is severely deaf. Hearing impairment results from three major factors that are not necessarily exclusive: environment, heredity, and old age.

Environmental causes include noise and accidental, toxic, and viral factors. Noise-induced deafness is primarily a phenomenon of the modern industrial world, though stonemasons, for example, may have been subject to hearing loss in the ancient world. Permanent deafness resulting from toxicity is also a phenomenon of the modern world. In contrast, deafness from accident, such as a blow to the ear, must have occurred from time to time. Various injuries resulted from boxing, including the "cauliflower ear." In fact, Aristophanes coined the term "ear-breaker" for a boxer.[3] A type of accident in which the ears themselves were injured is seen in an account by Plutarch of men whose noses and ears were mutilated as they were digging through Mount Athos (*Moralia* 470 e). While this tale is fantastic, designed to show an example of the Persian king Xerxes' hubris in cutting through Mount Athos, the detail of injured ears is believable.

Viruses, too, colonized the ancient world. Of the six main viruses that can cause deafness today—chickenpox, common cold viruses, influenza, measles, mumps, and poliomyelitis—there is evidence for all but measles in ancient Greece.[4] There is also evidence for the presence of bacterial meningitis, whose classic complication is hearing loss.[5] In modern, developed countries, preventive medicine reduces the incidence and severity of these viral and bacterial diseases, but in the ancient world, as in developing countries today, these viruses must have taken their toll. There is no record of any ancient Greek's experience of disease and consequent hearing loss; the humanity of the experience of losing one's hearing must be imagined.

There is no reason to rule out hereditary deafness in the ancient world, and there is some conjectural evidence for the other common results of inbreeding, although not specifically for deafness. Plutarch (*Moralia* 616 b) and Strabo (*Geography* 10.5.9.487 c), for example, observe the prevalence of premature baldness on the island of Mykonos. It is not surprising that island communities would have had their own genetic peculiarities. Genetic phenomena such as the present-day prevalence of female muteness on the island of Amorgos would have been common in ancient Greece.[6] Nora Groce gives an account of the island community of Martha's Vineyard, which until the twentieth century had a high proportion of people who were deaf as a result of inbreeding.[7] In addition to inbreeding, other hereditary factors can produce deafness. Some families simply have a genetic background that is predisposed to deafness. Furthermore, a chromosomal aberration can produce deafness, with or without a hereditary factor.[8] Today, one baby in one thousand is born profoundly deaf.[9]

Hearing loss is expected in elderly people in the modern world. Today, almost 30 percent of people sixty-five to seventy-four years old and almost 50 percent of those seventy to seventy-nine years old have some hearing loss; in other words, one-third of those over sixty-five have clinically abnormal hearing.[10] There is no reason to suppose that hearing loss would have been less a part of old age in the ancient world than it is today; if the incidence was similar, one Greek in three, sixty-five years or older, would have experienced some degree of hearing loss. Fewer people, on one hand, attained the age of sixty-five or older; on the other hand, "old age" began earlier in the ancient world.[11]

Finally, in addition to the three factors mentioned earlier, any condition that manifested in muteness would not have been differentiated from deafness by ancient Greeks. Even recently this has been the case. Donna Williams explains, in her account of her own autism, that she was "meaning-deaf" but, like many autistic children, was thought to be sound deaf.[12] Muteness can result from faulty information processing brought on by forms of autism, learning disabilities, and mental illness.

It is safe to assume, then, that there were deaf and hearing-impaired people of all ages in the ancient Greek world. The attitudes toward these people can be reconstructed from a variety of literary and nonliterary sources.

Although Herodotus's fanciful tale of two sons and a kingdom does not represent the proportion of deaf people in the ancient world, it is useful in that it illustrates two important ancient Greek assumptions about deaf people. First, and crucial to our understanding of the Greek concept of deafness, deafness typically involved muteness. The Lydian boy's deafness is the sole reason that Herodotus provides for his worthlessness, not because he could not hear but because he could not speak.[13] In this case, the word "deaf" (kôphos) encompasses both conditions; a deaf person was voiceless by nature, mute in the sense that the sea or the earth is mute, "stone deaf." "Stone deaf" is not an exclusively modern concept, though in the ancient world it was perhaps more literal. For example, a first- or second-century A.D. girl's grave stele from Smyrna, a Greek city on the west coast of Asia Minor, refers to the deaf stones of the tomb.[14]

The second and related assumption seen in Herodotus's tale is that muteness indicated diminished worth. Croesus's deaf son was incapacitated by his condition (Herodotus 1.34). It could not be clearer that the reason for the boy's uselessness was his deaf-muteness alone; in all other respects, Herodotus narrates, he was acceptable (Herodotus 1.85).[15] Croesus literally discounts his deaf son—"I do not count him as mine" (Herodotus 1.38). The parallels between discounting a "defective" child and discounting a female child are provocative and call to mind families who name only male children in census reports.[16] A deaf male child was perhaps as "worthless" as a girl, who, as shown in chapter 3, was thought to be constitutionally incapable of civic participation. Deafness certainly indicated worthlessness in the political sphere; this was so taken for granted that Herodotus uses it as a literary device: when Croesus's son finds his voice, Herodotus has created the irony that Croesus gained an heir when he lost his kingship.[17]

A survey of Classical uses of the word "deaf" (kôphos) shows that the term had a much wider range of meaning than the English term. Deafness and speechlessness were intertwined from the earliest appearance of the word, and the term does not always refer exclusively to a person's speech or hearing. In the *Iliad* (11.390), the term describes the bluntness of a weapon, the silence of an unbroken wave (14.16), and the muteness of the earth (24.54). This basic use of the word continues through the Archaic poets; for example, the seventh-century B.C. poet Alcman refers to a mute wave (frag. 14 c *PMG*).

The basic meaning of the word—blunt, dull, obtuse—took on a metaphorical meaning as well—dumb, mute, dull. When *kôphos* describes deafness as a human characteristic, it implies a range of conditions that include an overall inability to communicate verbally. The first surviving use of "deaf" that probably describes human beings appears in Aeschylus, though "my cry is to the deaf" could refer to anything that does not, or cannot, hear (*Libation Bearers* 881). There is a similar use when Eteocles asks the chorus of Theban women if he speaks to the deaf (*Seven against Thebes* 202).

The term unmistakably refers to a specific human sensory condition in the Hippocratic corpus, where it appears sixty-nine times. It is in the Hippocratic corpus, too, that the term first refers to a class of people.[18] There are two references to deaf people as a distinct group (*Coan Prognosis* 193.1; *Fleshes* 18.8).[19] As has been the case with other physical disabilities, most of the references are to deafness as a temporary condition, a symptom of another condition, or a diagnostic tool. Hippocratic writers rarely mention permanent deafness, as opposed to the temporary conditions such as "night deafness" that frequently accompany other ailments.[20] Deafness is mentioned in passing as a possible complication for the mother during childbirth, and muteness as a potential problem in the case of female hysteria.[21] The author of *Internal Affections* warns that deafness may result from a botched cauterization of one of the main veins in the body (18.24). A main vein, in Hippocratic thought, travels all the way from the head to the feet, and if it is severed in the area of the head, deafness or blindness results.

In short, throughout the Hippocratic corpus, deafness is seen more as a valuable diagnostic tool than as a physical infirmity in itself. There is not much surviving mention of medical treatment for deafness in the Classical period. Hippocratic theory was applied to Hellenistic practice in the writing of Celsus, who lived about six centuries after the earliest Hippocratic writers. In Celsus's writings, we see specific medical treatments for hearing impairment that are based on Hippocratic theory.[22] For example, there is a connection throughout the Hippocratic corpus between bilious bowels and deafness. We are told that, when bowels are bilious, deafness ensues (*Aphorisms* 4.28.1); furthermore, deafness accompanying a bowel movement full of black matter is fatal after a hemorrhage (*Prorrhetic* 1.129).[23] Celsus takes this connection another step in his recommendation to balance the humors by producing a bilious stool (2.8.19). Other remedies for ear ailments and times when the hearing gets dull include shaving the head, if the head is considered too heavy (6.7.7 b), and flushing the ear with various juices (6.7.8 a).[24]

Some of the more drastic treatments suggest to the modern reader that hearing impairments might have been aggravated or even caused by medical treatment, such as when a probe with turpentine-soaked wool was inserted into the ear and twisted around (6.7.9 a). This treatment is still successfully used today, as a solution of turpentine is helpful in loosening an impaction of ear wax; the danger lies, then and now, in inserting the probe too far and perforating the eardrum.

While the surviving medical literature of the Classical period does not include treatments for deafness, we do find reports of cures for deafness in the nonmedical literature. For example, psychological trauma instantly restored Croesus's son's capacity to speak (Herodotus 1.85), and a fourth-century B.C. inscription at Epidaurus testifies to a spontaneous cure of muteness.[25] Such cures are typically considered miraculous; this one is listed among other cures such as the restoration of a lost eyeball and the disappearance of scars (*ACIT* 230–31).

Deafness is not a common ailment among the surviving literary testimonies of Asclepiadic cures, but the paucity of written evidence does not necessarily indicate that the Greeks did not seek cures for it. Because it is an abstract characteristic, deafness is not easily depicted in words or in clay and, like headache, is difficult to interpret in representation.[26] This difficulty of representation may explain the lack of reference to deafness or muteness in the surviving papyri; I have yet to see a reference to either. Physical characteristics are mentioned in the papyri, especially in the private documents, but usually as neutral attributes, such as scars, that identify people. A negative characteristic, such as not speaking, would have been inefficient identification.

Clay representations of human ears were prominent among the offerings of body parts at the healing temples, and many survive. They may or may not represent thank offerings or pleas for cures of deafness;

such offerings could also represent thank offerings or pleas for cures of ear infections.²⁷ The ear was, obviously, connected with hearing and thus communication and—in ancient thought—intelligence. By extension, the ear was for Aristotle also indicative of personality—he associates large, projecting ears with senseless chatter (*History of Animals* 1.11.492 a). Similarly, the second-century A.D. writer Athenaeus tells us that when Midas became deaf through his stupidity, he received the ears of an ass to match his "dumbness" (12.516 b).

Because deafness and muteness were intertwined, models of mouths or complete heads may just as well have represented deafness as ears.²⁸ But the ear was, certainly, the most obvious channel of hearing, listening, and understanding, and this is why it was important to have the ear of the god from whom one sought a favor. If one's prayer was heard, it was granted.²⁹ Having the god's ear was taken literally: some temples included depictions of gods' ears into which the suppliant could speak.³⁰

Against this background, it is possible to reconstruct generally some of the realities of deaf people's lives in the ancient Greek world. I will discuss people with mild hearing impairments; followed by those people who were more severely deaf but who still spoke; and, finally, people who were prelingually deaf.

People with partial hearing loss outnumber people with severe or profound deafness in the modern world, and there is no reason to think that the situation was different in the ancient world. Partial loss of hearing, because of the difficulty in verbal communication it brought on, implied partial loss of wit. Perhaps Aristophanes used hearing impairment as a comic vehicle: the slave Demosthenes describes his master as a bit hard of hearing, quick tempered, and country minded (*Knights* 43).³¹ As in the modern world, old people were expected to become slightly deaf. Slight deafness was the "old man's forfeit," along with a decrease in sight, wit, and memory, according to the fourth-century B.C. historian Xenophon (*Memorabilia* 4.7.8). Old men and deafness were so intertwined that it is difficult to separate deafness from old age as the butt of the joke in Attic comedy.³² Aristophanes' Acharnian men contrast the city's brash and forensically skilled youth with their own deafness (*Acharnians* 681). The deafness here is literal, but it reveals layers of symbolism in the conflict of generations.³³ A diminished ability to communicate by speech accompanies hearing loss; the assumption of faulty thought accompanies this diminished ability to communicate easily; the picture of dull-witted old age results.

What this picture of diminished intellect meant in the everyday life of someone with a mild hearing impairment is impossible to determine in any great detail. Hard-of-hearing old men, though portrayed comically, are never portrayed—at least in the surviving material—as "worthless." As we have seen, an important measure of a Greek man's worth was his participation in the army or, at Athens, in the navy. Old men were not excluded from the hoplite forces. All citizens, regardless of age or physical fitness, were included in the military.[34] Of these old men, a significant proportion—upward of 30 percent, we have noted—must have been hearing impaired to some degree. This could even have worked to their advantage in the noisy confusion of Greek combat, where panic could quickly scatter the phalanx.[35]

As scant as the information is for deaf and hearing-impaired men, there is even less information about women.[36] An epigram from the first century A.D. describes a very deaf old woman who when asked to bring cheeses (*turos*) brings grain (*puros*) instead. "In fact," the narrator says, "she does not comprehend a word I say" (*Greek Anthology* 11.74). This is the only significant instance of a deaf woman that I have found in the Greek material. Silence in a woman was virtuous, and as we have seen in chapter 3, women's speech was, at best, less valuable than men's speech.[37] While the epigram on its own tells us little about deaf women, it does further illustrate the connection among deafness, old age, and impaired communication.

The degree of one's hearing loss never appears to have been an important issue; what mattered to the Greeks was one's ability to speak.[38] Even profoundly deaf people who learn spoken language before losing their hearing do not necessarily lose their capacity to speak. When Pseudo-Aristotle asks why deaf people talk through their noses, he refers to people who remember how to speak, but who do not remember how to regulate their voices (*Problems* 962 b).[39] Being able to speak intelligibly, even if imperfectly, separated mute people—the "dumb"—from those who merely had variations of speech, though the philosophical line was thin. Pseudo-Aristotle compares speech disorders with muteness: he asks why man is the only animal that stammers and asks in answer if it is because only man suffers from muteness and stammering is a form of muteness (*Problems* 895 a). Chapter 3 discussed the portrayals of people with imperfect speech. Their speech was ridiculed (Plutarch *Demosthenes* 4.8) or admired (Plutarch *Alcibiades* 1.4), but there is nothing to indicate the degree of derision seen in the story of Croesus's son.

Some deaf people did not learn spoken language. About one in one thousand people in the world today are congenitally deaf, and, given the etiology of deafness discussed earlier, there is no reason to believe that the proportion was much different in the ancient world.[40] In the absence of modern educational methods, one must hear spoken language in order to learn to speak it.[41] People in the ancient world who became deaf in utero or before learning to speak were necessarily mute.

Of course, prelingually deaf people who could not talk communicated in other ways; speech is only part of the method by which even people with full hearing transmit information.[42] Alan Boegehold, in his study of gesture in Greek literature, finds "a world in which gesture and posture were essential elements of communication."[43] Deaf children who are not taught a signed language naturally learn a system of gestures.[44]

While all language involves gesture, a system of gestures does not necessarily constitute a language, though William Stokoe argues that all language *is* gesture.[45] Conditions for a true, signed language would have been present only in areas in which deaf people interacted. In America, deafness goes beyond a physical disability to include a set of attitudes and behaviors: the shared experience based on a visual culture is one of the elements that creates a community among Deaf people.[46] Whether or not a deaf community existed anywhere in the ancient Greek world is impossible to determine, though one imagines that at least in the rural areas of Greece, there were only isolated deaf individuals. Furthermore, it is important to distinguish between early communities of deaf people and the newer, radical element of the Deaf community, which emerged from the Deaf Power Movement in the 1970s, when deaf people began to recognize themselves as a minority with a cultural heritage. In any case, any such area in Greece would have had to include adults who could teach sign language and an ongoing need to use the language. While deaf children in hearing families develop the skills necessary to learn sign language, a sign language does not materialize on its own, even between deaf peers. Sign language must be taught by someone proficient in it.[47]

Highly populated urban areas such as Athens and, especially, island communities that had a high incidence of hereditary deafness may have included generations of deaf people who used some form of sign language. Still, even if in Athens, with the largest population of any Greek polis by far, there were 60,000 citizens around 500 B.C., only 60 citizens would have been congenitally deaf.[48] The category of "citizens" includes male residents eligible to vote and does not include women, children, slaves, or foreign residents. If we double the population figure to include women, and double it again to include two children for each family, we still have only 240 congenitally deaf people up and down Attica, with no particular reason to be aware of each other's presence, especially given the lack of public schools. In a smaller community such as the island of Melos, with its fifth-century population of about 1,250 citizens, approximately 1 or 2 citizens and 5 people altogether would have been congenitally deaf.[49]

There is no proof of the presence, or the absence, of ancient Greek sign language. Someone signing language looks like someone gesturing. The handful of references to the gestures used by deaf people is inconclusive. Xenophon describes soldiers with a language barrier using gestures as if mute (*Anabasis* 4.5.33). Ctesias, a fifth-century doctor whose works survive only in fragments, refers to using signs like "the deaf and speechless" do (*FGrH* 688 F 45). Plato has Socrates suggest communication by gesture, "as mute men" (*Cratylus* 422 d–e). A Greek would not have differentiated between gestured communication and true sign language.

People who had learned writing before becoming deaf would have been able to use the written word to communicate. Such people would not have been common, though, as much of the population of the ancient Greek world was not merely illiterate (unable to write within a culture of writing) but nonliterate (unable to write, but within a culture in which written skills were an exception).[50] Furthermore, among children, the written word as a means of communication would have been limited to the rare family that included both parents who had mastered fluency of writing and reading and deaf children. Of course, the written language was not the only medium by which people who could not talk could transmit information. In the folk tale of the sisters Procne and Philomela, in which Procne's husband, Tereus, cuts out Philomela's tongue in order to prevent her from telling anyone that he raped her, Philomela weaves scenes into her tapestry that depict her story.[51]

Speaking Greek was a means of showing Greek identity as opposed to being considered a barbarian. Generally, people who did not speak Greek and who, for whatever reason, had to rely on gestured communication, were not admired. For example, Clytemnestra, in Aeschylus's *Agamemnon*, commands an unresponsive Cassandra, "Speak not, but make with your barbarian hand some sign" (1060–61). Similarly, the Phrygian messenger in Euripides' *Orestes*, both foreign and terrified, delivers his barely coherent report by pantomime, to the impatience and disgust of his audience (1369–1526). Furthermore, the inability to speak went beyond a simple barrier in communication. Aristotle observes that all people born deaf are also mute (*History of Animals* 4.9.536 b).[52] By "mute," Aristotle refers to an inability to express language, not an inability to form sounds. Babies who are born deaf, after all, still cry. Aristotle observes that animals make noise; human beings speak, and though people who are born deaf can make noise, they cannot talk (*History of Animals* 4.9.536 b). For the Greeks, as for all pre-Enlightenment cultures, speech, language, and reason were intertwined.[53] Because the conditions (inability to hear) and symptoms (inability to speak) of deafness were indistinct, Herodotus can use "deaf" and "speechless" interchangeably. As Herodotus's audience took for granted, deafness was synonymous with "dumbness" in its full range of meanings.

As embodied in the words of Isocrates, language was the hallmark of human achievement:

> And Athens it is that has honored eloquence, which men all crave and envy in its possessors; for she realized that this is the one endowment of our nature which singles us out from all living creatures, and that by using this advantage we have risen above them in all other respects as well; she saw that in other activities the fortunes of life are so capricious that in them often the wise fail and the foolish succeed, whereas beautiful and artistic speech is never allotted to ordinary men, but is the work of an intelligent mind, and it is in this respect that those who are accounted wise and ignorant present the strongest contrast. (*Panegyricus* 48)[54]

Muteness went beyond a physical condition. An inability to speak went hand in hand with an inability to reason, hand in hand with stupidity, embodied even today in the expression "deaf and dumb." Plato has Socrates say that anyone can show what he thinks about anything, unless he is speechless or deaf from birth (*Theaetetus* 206 d). The proverb recorded by Plutarch that states that only the oracle can understand the deaf further highlights the difficulty faced by people unable to communicate verbally (*Moralia* 512 d).

That muteness was seen as a grave affliction can be traced with three literary examples from the seventh century through the first century B.C. Hesiod describes the punishment for perfidious gods as a sort of temporary death, in which the god must lie for a year without breath, without voice (*Theogony* 793–98). In the chilling final scene of the *Alcestis*, the woman whom Heracles offers to Admetus is not dead yet not quite alive, Alcestis yet not quite Alcestis.[55] The emblem of this liminal state is her muteness (Euripides *Alcestis* 1143). Finally, Diodorus, in his account of Heracles' travels, reports that the punishment for the young men who failed to carry out sacred rites in honor of Iolaüs, Heracles' companion in his labors, was that they were struck mute and thus, he writes, resemble dead men (4.24.4–5).

Deafness was indeed a curse, sometimes literally. The word "deaf" appears in the surviving Greek inscriptions almost exclusively as a curse, and a powerful one. Deprivation of hearing, because it meant a deprivation of verbal communication and perceived intelligence, meant separation from the political and intellectual arena. A curse of deafness was appropriate not only for one's political opponents, whose speech could harm, but also for anyone who had too much power— many curse tablets are aimed at litigants. A tablet from the Athenian port of Piraeus of unknown date, for example, specifically requests speechlessness when a woman's tongue is cursed to be bound, made of lead, *and* stabbed.[56] Aristophanes provides a comedic example of this curse when the chorus teases Strepsiades, saying that he will wish his son, soon to be diabolically forensically skilled, were mute (*Clouds* 1320). This is reminiscent of the wisdom that the priestess at the Delphic oracle gives Croesus: such a horrible event—the imminent immolation of Croesus—will trigger his son's voice that it is better, she says, that his son remain mute (Herodotus 1.85).

In trying to reconstruct the daily realities of deaf people from scraps of information, the most substantial of which is Herodotus's tale, it is worth considering that concerns surrounding speech and intelligence were different for the literate elite than they were for the bulk of the population, but that we rely on the literate elite for almost all our information about deafness. The elite valued the very skills—such as fluency in communication—that they thought deaf people lacked. Herodotus's

Greek audience knew that Croesus's son could never become king. Aristotle and his circle had the luxury of despising lack of eloquence, but the average peasant would have been far less concerned with a child's forensic skills. The deaf child of a farmer or shepherd, even if considered utterly stupid and incapable of political activity, could certainly have carried out any number of tasks.[57]

In summary, we are confined to learning about deafness in the ancient Greek world through the filter by which the information was transmitted. In other words, the most closely we can observe everyday life for deaf people is through a partial reconstruction of attitudes toward deaf people. Life in Greece for anyone who did not speak must have been frustrating occasionally. But while the consequences of deafness are synonymous with exile or death in the literature, it is important to remember that more people in the Greek world were interested in farming than in rhetoric; that is, the majority of the population was composed of peasant farmers, not politicians. Limited conversational ability among peasants might have been a frustration, but not an insurmountable condition. While ineligibility in political and intellectual arenas may have been a hardship for some, the hardship is magnified out of proportion in the surviving material. Once again we are reminded to resist the tendency to read modern values about physical disability into ancient material or to assume modern values about intellectual capabilities.

5   Degrees of Sight and Blindness   ∾

The blind bard Homer, the blind seer Teiresias, and Oedipus Rex, who
was blinded by divine punishment, dominate most discussions of
blindness in the ancient Greek world. By supplying an apparent historical precedent, generalizations made from the tales of these figures support modern attitudes toward blindness and blind people, such as the
idea that blind people are special but horrifying. While mention of
blindness is found in the myth, epic, and tragedy that relate the stories
of the three famous blind figures, it is fallacious to transfer attitudes
seen in the grand sweep of legend and tragedy to everyday life and to
generalize that "many Greeks viewed blindness as a fate worse than
death. They saw blindness as a punishment from the gods." Herbert C.
Covey, who made this comment in a 1998 survey of blind people
through history, continues: "This basic belief provided a rationaliza-
tion for negative social practices and attitudes toward people with
blindness in Greek society."[1] Negative social practices and attitudes
toward blindness abound in modern, developed society, but there is
not enough relevant information to make similar conclusions about
ancient Greek society. Covey's statement is just one example of the
prevalent notion about the plight of blind people in ancient Greece.[2]

In this chapter, I argue that the story of blind people in the ancient
Greek world is neither glorious nor dismal and that blind people were
far from exceptional. There were many ways to lose one's vision, and
there were many sight-impaired people. The potential that one could
lose one's sight was a simple fact of life. Anxiety over vision is reflected
in stories about sudden and permanent blindness, and these are the

stories that have survived. Stories about ordinary people with vision gradually fading from cataracts are not the stuff of legend. Similarly, the fact that a blind person can live an ordinary life by relying on senses other than sight is not particularly interesting; divine compensation such as the gift of extraordinary hearing makes a more durable tale. Some blind people were venerated; some were castigated; most went about their business, albeit with more difficulty and physical vulnerability than a sighted person, and are lost from the record.

In developed countries, we take near-perfect sight, naturally or by correction, for granted. William Paulson, in *Enlightenment, Romanticism, and the Blind in France,* points out that blindness is not a phenomenon that exists independently; rather, its definition and meaning are determined by any given culture.[3] Indeed, the parameters of blindness and the relationship between blindness and sight impairment were perceived differently in the Greek world than in the modern world. In the United States today, for example, a person who can perceive light and shape may nevertheless be categorized as completely blind; a person who can read to some extent might be legally blind.[4] There were, of course, no measurements for vision in the Greek world and no serviceable corrective lenses.[5] The criteria for what constituted blindness were stricter in the ancient world, as the Greek vocabulary suggests.

From the first appearance in the *Iliad* of the most common term for a blind person (*tuphlos*), the term refers to someone who has no sight at all (6.139).[6] Aristotle, who pairs blindness and sight as fundamental opposites (*Categories* 10.11 b 24), implies that this absolute blindness is permanent when he states that someone who has become blind never regains his sight (*Categories* 13 a).[7] As today, the term "blind" (*tuphlos*) is used broadly. It refers to both physical and moral blindness, which is what allowed Sophocles to play with the term when he calls King Creon blind in his craft of rulership and has the seer Teiresias refer to his own, literal blindness (*Oedipus the King* 388–89, 412–13). It also refers to figurative blindness such as blind wealth, most obviously seen in Aristophanes' play *Wealth* (13, 15, 48, 90, 301, inter alia), and blind love (Plato *Laws* 731 d–e; Plutarch *Moralia* 90 a, 92 e, 1000 a, inter alia). The term is also used figuratively in the expression "blind alley."[8] An equivalent, less common term for blindness (*alaos*) is first evident in the *Odyssey* (8.195, 10.493, 12.267). This term is, for example, what Sophocles uses when the chorus asks Oedipus if he had been born blind (*Oedipus at Colonus* 148–49). Another term for "blind" (*atê*) originally referred to physical blindness, and this meaning is retained in the Homeric writings, but refers to metaphorical blindness in post-Homeric literature.[9]

The difference between the Greek and the modern criteria for blindness is highlighted by the ancient term for dull-sightedness (*ambluôpia*), which refers to anyone who does not see well, but who is not actually blind. Plato calls dull-sightedness simply a faultiness of the eyes (*Hippias Minor* 374 d 2). Galen groups together weakness in an eye and dull-sightedness (12.533.4–5). Plutarch shows that one could be extremely dull-sighted yet not, by ancient standards, blind. Flatterers, he writes, in his guide to etiquette, imitate their host by pretending to take on whatever handicap the host has. They pretend to see indistinctly, for instance, if their host is partially blind (*hupotuphlos*), as was the case with a certain Dionysius, who was dull-sighted.[10] Dionysius was so dull-sighted that his guests, in imitation, bumped into each other and knocked around the dishes (*Moralia* 53 f).

From the earliest appearance of blindness in Greek mythology, in which the mythical musician Thamyris is blinded by the Muses for his attempts to rival their musical skills, blinding is presented as a divine punishment (Homer *Iliad* 2.594–600).[11] One might get the impression "that Greece and Rome must have had a large population of blind people, most of them blinded by force as punishment for some misdeed or defeat in war."[12] While the ancient world must indeed have had a large population of blind people, and while trauma was certainly responsible for some sight impairment, the proportion of people who were blind from accident as opposed to those blind from disease must have been small. Even today, with such phenomena as automobiles, guns, and power tools, trauma is the cause of only 2.9 percent of legal blindness in the United States.[13] Nevertheless, three causes of traumatic blinding—revenge, industrial accident, and battle—are apparent in the literature, though in most cases the literature is mythological rather than historical.

First, traumatic blinding as a result of divine or mortal revenge is dramatic and appears in several tales. Zeus in his anger blinds the Thracian king Lycurgus (Homer *Iliad* 6.138–40); in order to escape, Odysseus blinds his captor, the cyclops Polyphemus, in one heroic lunge (Homer *Odyssey* 9.382–94). Plato recounts the Archaic poet Steisichorus's divine blinding as punishment for slandering Helen (*Phaedrus* 243). The Thracian king Phineus, who had blinded his stepsons (Apollodorus 3.15.2–3), was in turn blinded by the Argonauts, according to Apollodorus (1.9.21) and Diodorus (4.44.4); in Sophocles' *Antigone*, Phineus's sons were blinded by their stepmother in one stroke of her shuttle (974–76).[14] Finally, Achilles' companion Phoenix's blinding at the hands of his father is recounted by Apollodorus (3.13.8).

Perhaps this mythological tradition of divine blinding as punishment reflects human practice, though historical accounts of blindings as punishment at the hands of mortals are also fanciful. Herodotus tells the tale of Evenius, blinded by others of his village as punishment for his failure to tend the sacred sheep (9.93). Plutarch paints the gruesome picture of the caged Telesphorus, with his eyes—and most other extremities—cut out by the Hellenistic King Lysimachus, under whom he had served (*Moralia* 606 b); Athenaeus adds that this was Telesphorus's punishment for having joked about Lysimachus's wife (14.616 c). Other fanciful, mythological examples of blindings by mortal hands include Odysseus's blinding of Polyphemus, mentioned earlier. The swiftness in the Homeric version is reversed for comic effect in Euripides' version of the slow, bumbling, cowardly blinding in the *Cyclops* (590–665). Oedipus's is the most memorable and gruesome blinding of them all. The messenger narrates that Oedipus tore the golden pins from his dead wife's clothes

> And raised them up, and struck his own eyeballs,
> Shouting words such as these "No more shall you
> Behold the evils I have suffered and done.
> Be dark from now on, since you saw before
> What you should not, and knew not what you should."
> Moaning such cries, not once but many times,
> He raised and struck his eyes. The bloody pupils
> Bedewed his beard. The gore oozed not in drops,
> But poured in a black shower, a hail of blood.
> (Sophocles *Oedipus the King* 1269–79)[15]

Industrial accident, the second cause of traumatic blinding, makes a less dramatic tale than revenge. Herodotus reports that the Cnidians, while breaking stones in the process of digging across an isthmus, were wounded in their eyes (1.174). While the especially frequent wounds in this case were, Herodotus tells us, a divine warning, quarrying, along with masonry, mining, and smithing, must have been a dangerous endeavor that sometimes resulted in eye injuries. That blind people were especially selected to work in mines, as suggested by modern scholars, is not documented in the Greek material.[16]

Third, battlefield accidents also accounted for some traumatic blinding. We have the memorable Homeric scene, for example, of the warrior Peisander's eyeballs falling before Menelaus's feet (*Iliad* 13.616–18). In this case, Peisander did not survive; nevertheless, the scene illustrates a familiarity with eye loss through battle trauma. Another sort of blindness acquired in the military setting is seen where Herodotus tells of Epizelus the Athenian, who became suddenly blind at the Battle of Marathon after seeing a vision (6.117).[17] A fourth-century inscription at the Asclepiadic healing temple at Epidaurus tells of the otherwise unknown Anticrates of Cnidus, who, during battle, had been hit by a spear in both eyes and sought a cure for the resulting blindness (*ACIT* 235).[18]

While miraculous cures such as Anticrates' cannot be explained in rational terms, the tale is valuable in that it demonstrates that the line between sight and blindness was more fluid in the ancient world than in our own. Perhaps this fluidity was a result of the ancient lack of measurement for sight combined with the lack of detailed anatomical knowledge. As an example of the difference between the ancient and the modern perception of blindness and its potential cure, it is now known that a deficiency in vitamin A can cause nutritional blindness, a reversible condition that sometimes manifests as night blindness.[19] It may have been nutritional blindness that affected the fourth-century Athenian statesman Demetrius of Phalerum, who, we are told by Diogenes Laertius, became blind in Alexandria, then recovered his sight through the favor of Sarapis, a god of healing powers (*Demetrius* 76). Another case of reversible blindness is seen in an inscription at the healing site at Epidaurus. It tells of a certain Hermon of Thasos, who was first cured of his blindness and then, when he failed to thank the god properly, was blinded again. Hermon was finally cured when he righted his wrong (*ACIT* 233–34).[20]

People with nutritional blindness who sought cures at the healing temples may have partaken of an animal sacrifice and thus ingested a dose of vitamin A sufficient to alleviate the blindness.[21] Although the nutritional science behind the cure was not understood, a Hippocratic doctor does prescribe eating a large amount of beef liver once or twice a day as a treatment for night blindness (*On Vision* 9.7), and Galen recommends eating a lot of roasted goat liver to cure night blindness (12.802–3).[22]

Far more than traumatic injury, however, disease was responsible for most blindness and sight impairment. Cataract, a disease that clouds the usually transparent lens structure, is the major cause of blindness in the modern world, and there is no reason to rule it out as a major cause of blindness in the ancient world.[23] Cataract strikes people of all ages, and no one is immune to age-related cataract. Hippocratic writers observed and reported the condition (*On Vision* 9.4–5); later medical writers such as Galen recorded their attempts at surgical treatment of it (10.990).[24] We see, in a private letter of the fourth century A.D. (*P. Oxy.* 31.2601), what must have been a common situation: a person with "white eyes" (*leukeumatiôn*)—a perfect description of cataracts—is urged to travel from the village to the city for a cure.

Glaucoma, the second major cause of blindness next to cataracts in the modern world, may also have been a major cause of blindness in the ancient world. Glaucoma results from extreme, sustained pressure in the eyeball, eventually leading to blindness. A Hippocratic writer could be describing advanced glaucoma when he discusses an eye infection that causes inflammation and rupture of the eyes (*Airs Waters and Places* 2.4).[25]

Prenatal influence, including heredity, is the major reason that people acquire cataracts and glaucoma, as well as other eye problems. The phenomenon of hereditary sight impairment is recorded by Plutarch, who tells us that Timoleon, the Corinthian general who liberated Syracuse in the fourth century B.C., slowly became blind from an inherited eye weakness (*Timoleon* 37.6–7). While we will never know exactly what sight impairment Timoleon had, we do know that a predisposition for cataracts as well as glaucoma can be inherited. Ancient Greek authors guessed that some families were more prone than others to sight loss and observed that blind parents sometimes produced blind babies (*Sacred Disease* 6.2 9; Aristotle *History of Animals* 585 b). Another suggestion of inherited blindness is seen in a tale of Diodorus in which a king's son loses his sight because he shares his father's constitution (1.59.1–4). This conclusion follows from simple observation, of course, not an underlying understanding of genetics.

Whether or not babies born blind were subject to exposure is another matter. Some survived, or the chorus's question to Oedipus, "Were you blind from birth?," would not make sense (Sophocles *Oedi-*

pus at Colonus 148–49). Similarly, Aristotle refers to a man born blind (*Physics* 193 a). Furthermore, even if parents would have preferred to be rid of blind offspring, it is difficult to determine whether or not an infant will be permanently blind. Even if the infant had visibly mutilated eyes, Greek parents may have held hope for a cure. We have the remarkable testimony (*ACIT* 231–32) of a man so blind that one of his eye sockets was completely empty, yet full sight was restored. While few people in the modern world would accept such a cure as true, people in the ancient world were not as tied as we are to rational explanation. Pliny observes that humans alone, as opposed to animals, are cured of blindness by the emission of fluid from their eyes; he cites a case of a man's cure after having been blind for twenty years (*Natural History* 11.55.149).

Though it does not appear much in Greek legend, eye disease was a common complaint in the ancient world. Along with cataract and glaucoma, contagious disease, in an age without vaccinations, antibiotics, or infection control, was responsible for damage to the eyes.[26] Galen mentions 124 pathological conditions of the eye (12.766–77).[27] We can only guess at the exact disease that manifests in the Hippocratic corpus as discharges that ulcerate the eyelids and eat the covering of the eyeball, but we do know the general categories of maladies that existed (*Ancient Medicine* 1.19). There is evidence for the existence of bacterial infections, such as staphylococcal; viral infections, such as smallpox; and fungal infections, such as *Candida*.[28] All of these infections have devastating effects on the eye in any environment without, for example, penicillin. Eye diseases such as the viral disease trachoma, which Galen discusses (12.709), are highly contagious, flourishing in poor economic conditions and where poor personal hygiene exists. Untreated trachoma can destroy the eyeballs completely.[29] Today, antibiotics keep infectious eye disease under control in developed countries, but eye infections flourished in ancient Greece, as reflected both by the Hippocratic medical texts (e.g., *On Vision* 9.6) and by clay models of eyes. These clay representations of eyes, found at the healing sites of the god Asclepius, may represent preventative measures against eye disease or pleas or thanks for cures of eye disease.[30] Clay models and other depictions of eyes are not uncommon; the most remarkable site is the Athenian Asclepion, where an inscription includes 154 representations of eyes (13 single, 141 pairs), dedicated between the mid–fourth and third centuries B.C. This is a large number; either eyes in such quantities are missing from other inventories, or visual problems were especially prevalent in Athens in the mid–third century B.C.[31] It could be, too, that certain temples came to have reputations for healing certain conditions.

Epidemic infection also caused blindness and sight impairment. Thucydides' details of the Athenian plague of 429 B.C. include his observation that many of the survivors lost their eyes (2.49.8).[32] Although Thucydides could mean that the survivors lost their sight, they may have actually lost part of their eyeballs; either way, the point remains. Of course, this was not the only instance of this particular epidemic, and it was certainly not the only plague. Dangerous epidemic disease was common in the Graeco-Roman world.[33] A Hippocratic writer, for example, observes annual and epidemic outbreaks of ophthalmia (*On Vision* 9.9).

Finally, failing eyesight came with old age. Xenophon includes diminished sight in his "old man's forfeit" (*Memorabilia* 4.7.8). The physiology of sight, while explored by the Hippocratic practitioners, was not fully understood. Greek scientists, for example, considered blue eyes a pathological phenomenon.[34] Nevertheless, the eyeball was sensibly perceived as an aqueous entity that had to be the perfect mixture of wet and dry. Aristotle explains that one should not have too much or too little fluid in eyes; the best sight of all results when there is neither too little nor too much. He also notes that some eyes are less visually acute than others, especially blue eyes, because they are deficient in water (*Generation of Animals* 779 b).[35] As a person ages and loses his moisture, Aristotle explains further, the eyeballs naturally dry up and become hardened (*Generation of Animals* 780 a).

Between trauma, heredity, unchecked contagious disease, and old age, we can infer that blindness and sight impairment such as extreme myopia were common in ancient Greece. This is not surprising, nor is it surprising that there is a fair amount of reference to sight and blindness in Greek literature.[36] References to blind people in folklore and mythology, though, no matter how numerous, do not supply much direct information about the everyday realities for blind and sight-impaired humans. Nevertheless, we can gather some information indirectly, and in broad outline, about religious attitudes toward blindness and daily life for ordinary blind people, as well as some facets of their economic and military roles.

Aristotle writes that sight is the most important sense of all (*On the*

Senses 437 a). Blindness in myth is a punishment, a metaphor for ignorance, isolation, and death.[37] Blindness was never something to desire. But that blind people were routinely associated with evil, that "a person with a squint or a cataract would be considered to have the signs of the evil eye," is not borne out by the Greek sources.[38] It does not ring true to imagine that a familiar member of a community, such as a shopkeeper or a shoemaker, would have been considered magically evil when he began to suffer from glaucoma or cataracts.

On the other side of the coin, although myth shows divine compensation for blindness, I cannot imagine that the average Greek with progressively worsening cataracts would seriously have been waiting for his ration of clairvoyance and musical talent. Still, blindness was a common enough condition, to which people could and did adjust. The adjustment could not have been easy, especially the very early adjustment and especially in the case of a sudden onset of blindness. Euripides comically portrays the slapstick clumsiness of the newly blinded Polyphemus (*Cyclops* 660 ff) and portrays the same clumsiness tragically in the *Hecuba* (1056–57).

Yet people who lose their sight learn to rely more on their hearing, which in the ancient world may have been better, in general, than in the present.[39] The blind person's ordinary reliance on hearing becomes exaggerated in Greek mythology to an extraordinary range of hearing, so keen that the divine language of birds can be understood. In the case of Teiresias, Athena cleaned his ears so thoroughly after he was blinded that he could not only hear but also understand the notes of birds (Apollodorus 3.6.7). On one hand, it is mistaken to assume that blind people have superhuman senses of hearing, smell, or extrasensory perception, the premise of the 1992 film *Scent of a Woman*.[40] The themes of blindness and insight, "the use of metaphors embodying light and illumination, and their opposites," are common in myth and literature but have very little to do with the daily activities of real blind people.[41] Kathi Wolfe plays on this assumption in a satirical essay in which she reports being patronized by a woman who asks inappropriate questions about her blindness ("how in the world do you wash your underwear?"). Wolfe finds herself weaving a tale of her career as the world's first blind entomologist: "What convinced my colleagues that I could do the job was my ability to hear insect noises barely audible to sighted people. Could you distinguish between the hum of a yellow cicada and the hiss of the blue-legged centipede?"[42] Of course, people without sight do *learn* to use other senses, and this reality is what gets exaggerated in Greek myth—and present-day misunderstanding—as a superhuman gift.[43]

Relying on senses other than sight, blind people can adjust to their environment and maneuver capably, especially in familiar territory. A 1995 study of elderly blind people found that the only tasks with a high index of difficulty were sight-intensive tasks such as sewing and knitting. "Walking on a level surface" was rated at 1.7, with 1 corresponding to "can do very easily" and 5 corresponding to "can't do at all."[44] Teiresias's special staff, with which, Apollodorus writes, he got around as well as a sighted person, perhaps reflects a view of blind people navigating successfully with the help of a stick (3.6.7). Teiresias's blindness seems merely an excuse for stage directions in Euripides' *Bacchae* (192). He is plenty nimble, despite his blindness and his age: he refuses the cart that Cadmus suggests they take up the mountain.

In the mythological setting, blind people are usually guided by other people. Teiresias is led along the road by his slave (Sophocles *Antigone* 910–11). Another example of a sighted person's guiding a blind person is a herald leading the prototype of the blind bard, Demodocus, into the revelry of Odysseus's hosts, the Phaeacaeans, and leading him away again (Homer *Odyssey* 8.62, 106). Sophocles' Oedipus is unable, without sight, to move without a hand to guide him (*Oedipus at Colonus* 495–502). Oedipus refers to Antigone's hands as staffs and to her eyes as his eyes (*Oedipus at Colonus* 848, 866–67).[45] This pitiful vision of a mature, broken man relying on a young, devoted woman for his most basic needs is depicted and reinforced by images such as those in the early nineteenth-century *Oedipus and Antigone at Colonus* of Johann Peter Krafft (fig. 5).[46]

The contrast between being home and being abroad was very strong in the ancient world. Teiresias, Demodocus, and Oedipus were in dramatically unfamiliar territory: Oedipus, for example, was in exile. Most people in the ancient Greek world did not often have occasion to walk unfamiliar roads, but lived in one area all their lives. Travel was not pleasant or easy, and one would have traveled for specific goals only.[47] In one's own environment, one would have been able to maneuver easily. In an ancient Greek village, especially, the complicated and static topography would have provided excellent landmarks for a blind person. John Hull, a professor of religious education at the University of Birmingham, who is blind, explains the horror of wide-open, flat

Krafft portrays Oedipus as a broken man relying on his devoted daughter for his
needs. While the pathos of the scene may be timeless, blindness was not necessarily a pitiful situation in the lives of ordinary Greeks. Johann Peter Krafft
(1780–1856), *Oedipus and Antigone at Colonus,* pen and brown ink, brush and
brown wash over graphite on off-white wove paper, 46.5 × 34.6 cm., inv. no.
89.65. The Minneapolis Institute of Arts.

spaces: it is much easier for a blind person to know where he is by a varied topography. Hills and valleys, low walls, and many changes in texture constitute orienting signals.[48] So as not to idealize the ancient village, it should be pointed out that the presence of litter and feral dogs would not have been ideal for a blind person's navigation. I have come across no reference to dogs as guides for blind people, which is surprising, as dogs in the Greek world were devoted companions.[49] Of course, the lack of reference does not indicate an absence of guide dogs.

In any case, the allure of mobility and of personal independence, and the corresponding shame of relying on other people for basic needs, are modern notions, reinforced by the medical system.[50] Interdependence might better describe the ancient relationship of an individual within his own family and community.[51] In Greek literature, it is indeed pitiable to be weak, old, and newly blinded, while having to navigate through a foreign place. The chorus's assessment that Oedipus would be better off dead is not based on Oedipus's blindness alone, but on his blindness in exile and his choice to condemn himself to this fate (Sophocles *Oedipus the King* 1368, 1340–42). Similarly, Euripides' Polymestor in *Hecuba* is, like Oedipus, newly blind and not in his native land but away from home, which makes his blinding more poignant (1056–88).[52]

Indeed, most of the blind people in Greek mythology are extraordinary characters, such as beggars, prophets, bards, or some combination thereof. Demodocus the bard, for example, is dependent on the magnanimity of Odysseus for a piece of meat (Homer *Odyssey* 8.476–77). Blind people in literature often receive extraordinary gifts to match their extraordinary punishment, such as Teiresias (Homer *Odyssey* 10.493–95), Phineus (Apollodorus 1.9.21, 3.6.7), and Evenius (Herodotus 9.94). While the very earliest victims of divine blinding, in the *Iliad*, are not compensated by musical skills, they are nevertheless loosely associated with music and the Muses. Thamyris is punished with blindness *for* his skill in song (Homer *Iliad* 2.594–600); Lycurgus is blinded for tampering with Dionysus, god of wine and inspiration (Homer *Iliad* 6.139–40). Steisichorus was traditionally blinded and unblinded in connection with his poetry, as Plato relates (*Phaedrus* 243).

Still, it is dangerous to extract from myth conclusions about the consequences of blindness in daily life. Citing very little evidence, some scholars may have made sweeping generalizations about the status of blind people in the ancient world: "In ancient Greece some blind individuals were notable as poets, teachers, or fortune tellers. However, many were beggars, while others were segregated to perform repetitive tasks, including working in the mines."[53] In ordinary, mortal life, there probably were some blind singers and fortune-tellers, and some blind people did beg for their living, but these were not the only professions available.[54] There is no practical reason why a blind person would have been banned a priori from most occupations and no reason to agree with the conclusion of the author of a 1932 history of blindness that "want and suffering were the rule rather than the exception and the blind were an economic liability."[55]

We hear of blind scholars, for example, such as Didymus the Blind, from the fourth century A.D.[56] The third-century B.C. scholar Eratosthenes had dulling vision.[57] The Greeks believed Homer, their most revered author, to have been blind.[58] These are not necessarily exceptional cases. Our modern culture is very visually oriented, and relatively few people know blind people well. To some people who do not know blind people it might seem difficult to carry out scholarly work without sight, especially if the work involves the mathematical concepts with which Eratosthenes worked. Kathi Wolfe, in her essay "The Write Stuff," summarizes the obstacles she faced while fulfilling her lifelong ambition to be a writer in the phrase "blind girls can't write."[59] It is only in the modern world that we have come to link scholarship so tightly with the ability to read and write.[60] In the ancient world, wealthy scholars, at least, dictated to slaves, who did the actual writing.[61]

We see, between the lines of mythology, that it was not out of the question for blind people to participate in some agricultural activities. Polyphemus, even newly blinded, kept track of his sheep by running his hands over their backs as they left the cave and was astute enough to realize that they exited out of their usual order (Homer *Odyssey* 9.440–60). While this is a fanciful story within a fanciful story, a wrinkle that allows the Cyclops to voice his thoughts to the last-out ram, there is no reason to doubt the background information, that a blind shepherd knew his area, his wards, and their habits so well that he would not need sight to carry on his profession. Interestingly, Plutarch calls the Cyclops "a shepherd blinded" (*Moralia* 176 f). Herodotus relates the tale of the blinded Scythian slave milkers, and while the tale is fantastic, Herodotus's audience had to believe that

blind people could carry out tasks in a milking operation (4.2).[62] Evenius, punished by his neighbors with blindness, then compensated by
an offer of anything he wanted, chose the best plots of land in Apol-
lonia (Herodotus 9.94). Again, the tale is fantastic, but within the res-
olution of the tale is a blind man who owns a great deal of fertile land,
which suggests an underlying reality of blind people's economic participation in society.

Even if a blind man could participate in cultivating the land, he
could not take active part in battle. He could row a trireme, certainly,
but for the hand-to-hand combat on the front lines, at least some sight
was required. Some visual perception was necessary for the chaos of
hand-to-hand combat, especially because one would not have been
able to hear very well, between the noise of the battle and the muffling
effect of the helmet.[63] Apparently, though, even a little visual perception was adequate for front-line combat: Plutarch shows us Timoleon
taking part in active battle at an advanced age, although he suffered
from cataracts and was soon to be completely blind (*Timoleon* 37.6–8).
To be a real Greek man was to be a soldier. This is perhaps why Polybius calls a creature without eyesight "wholly useless" (*achreioutai to
holon*), as useless "as History stripped of truth" (1.14.6). Interestingly,
though, it is a few "useless men" (*achreiotatôn*) who Themistocles
thinks can hold the walls of the Piraeus during the Persian Wars
(Thucydides 1.93.6).[64] As we have seen, a class of noncombatants may
have existed at Athens, and a later example of the possible existence of
a special military class of physically disabled men is seen in a third-century A.D. Greek inscription from Memphis.[65] This inscription catego-
rizes young men who have been in military training into three groups,
one of which consists of those who "fall short in respect to eyesight."
In this case, the group was included in the ephebic corps by special dis-
pensation.[66] Since women, considered weak and inferior by nature,
sometimes participated in wartime activities such as preparing the
armor, repairing walls, and digging trenches, such support activities for
blind people cannot be ruled out.[67]

In conclusion, the Greeks' concept of vision had little to do with the
modern one. There was no measured scale of vision, from perfect sight
to legal blindness. One saw, even if only a little, or one did not see.
Either condition could be reversed in an instant. No one in the Greek
world was immune to blindness. Most of us in the developed world live
in the luxury of assuming that we will not—among other fates—

become blind. In the ancient world, it was perhaps more reasonable to assume that one would lose at least some of one's sight. It follows that in the ancient world, sighted people knew blind and sight-impaired people well enough to understand the abilities and limitations of failing vision and that there was not the cultural gulf between the sighted and the blind that exists today.

Greek myths and tales reflect truths and anxieties about sight and blindness in the ancient world. The tales of blind people come from the ancient, contextual understanding of what blindness meant. Blindness meant adapting one's life and activities to the individual's unique condition. In contrast, measurements and categories for degrees of vision determine one's legal status as a sighted or blind person in the modern, developed world. Blindness itself, regardless of individual circumstances, is seen as pitiful and tragic and, like any evident disability, overrides any other physical characteristic. Lynn Manning illustrates these principles in "The Magic Wand":

> Quick-change artist extraordinaire,
> I whip out my folded cane
> and change from black man to blind man
> with a flick of my wrist.
> It is a profound metamorphosis—
> From God-gifted wizard of roundball
> dominating backboards across America
> To God-gifted idiot savant
> pounding out chart-busters on a cock-eyed whim;
> From sociopathic gangbanger with death for eyes
> to all-seeing soul with saintly spirit;
> From rape driven misogynist
> to poor motherless child;
> From welfare-rich pimp
> to disability-rich gimp;
> And from "white man's burden"
> to every man's burden.
>
> It is always a profound metamorphosis,
> Whether from cursed by man to cursed by God;
> or from scripture-condemned to God-ordained,
> my final form is never of my choosing;
> I only wield the wand;
> You are the magician.

A blind person today, beyond simply having a physical disability to be accommodated under the ADA, takes on an identity steeped in fabricated ancient tradition. The quantitative modern understanding of blindness twists the ancient Greek tales of blindness as underpinnings for discrimination against blind people in the modern world.

Conclusions ∾

Moses I. Finley points out that because the elderly are not isolated from society, it is difficult to consider them separately.[1] This is the crux of the problem in looking at people with disabilities in Greek society. One of the reasons why it is difficult to find information about people with disabilities in Greek society is that they were integral to the society. There is no indication that people with physical handicaps in the ancient Greek world identified themselves or were identified as a distinct minority group, as is the case today.

Disabled people existed in great numbers, but discussing disability in categories is artificial. The organization of this book suggests that ancient Greeks would acquire one handicap or another, but never two or three. This, of course, is ridiculous, and the significance of being both deaf and blind, for example, must have had consequences that were greater than the sum of both handicaps.

I will conclude by presenting an Athenian court case from the fifth century B.C. that illustrates several points that I have made throughout the book about the place of people with physical disabilities in ancient Greek society. A critical Greek term, "unable" (*adunatos*), as it appears in Lysias 24, "On the Refusal of a Pension," highlights the differences between ancient society and modern, developed society. One must be aware of the dangers of misinterpreting this term, both to make sense of the speech of Lysias and to integrate the speech into the broader context of physical disability in ancient Greece.

Lysias 24 is likely a genuine speech both in authorship and in that it was meant for presentation—whether or not it actually was presented—before the Athenian Boule, the council that ran the affairs of state on behalf of the entire citizen body. The speech probably dates to the closing years of the fifth century.[2] The defendant, whose name we never learn, had been classed among the unable (*tôn adunatôn*) and had been receiving a state pension.

This pension is summarized in the Aristotelian *Athenian Constitution*. Each year, the Boule assesses the men who are classed as unable (*adunatous*). People in this class, who have very little wealth or who are physically impaired so as to be unable to work, receive a very small grant from the state.[3] This grant has been taken to indicate the humanitarian nature of the Athenian community. While not ruling out compassion, Matthew Dillon suggests that it was also a means to avoid aristocratic patronage, which leads to the tendency of the enfranchised poor to be in debt to aristocratic factions.[4]

The defendant is now accused of being able-bodied (*sômati dunasthai*) and carrying on a trade, thus being ineligible for the grant. Specifically, the defendant is charged with mounting and riding horses, carrying on a trade, and associating with wealthy friends (4–5).[5] Lysias composed this speech, in which the words of the defendant are in the first person, for the defendant to deliver before the Boule.

The defendant has a physical handicap. This handicap affects his mobility. Well into the speech, he mentions casually the two sticks on which he relies to walk (12). Furthermore, he is unable to walk long distances at all. We have seen that many people were physically handicapped and that having a handicap did not put one in any special category. Indeed, although the defendant has a significant mobility impairment, which might have consisted of anything from weak and gnarled legs to no legs at all—we are never told—he cannot simply display himself to the council to prove that he is indeed "unable." The members of the Boule know that he is handicapped; he stands before them on his two crutches. Furthermore, they've seen him around town; he's an old-timer, and he's been receiving the pension for years. Yet being visibly and permanently physically handicapped does not automatically make him unable (*adunatos*). When he refers to his bodily condition, he never uses the term "unable" (*adunatos*). He refers vaguely to "the afflictions of the body" and to the misfortune that makes it difficult for him to make long journeys, and he suggests sarcastically that it is he whose body is sound and that his accuser ought to be voted the maimed one.

People with physical handicaps were not necessarily barred from some roles. Material in earlier chapters shows that one could be significantly physically handicapped yet capable of supporting oneself; this is, after all, the claim the accuser is making against the defendant, and the charge is serious enough to merit a hearing before the Boule. Lysias has the defendant argue that he should be categorized as unable (*adunatos*), not on grounds that he can barely walk but rather for three other reasons: a father who left him nothing, an aged mother whom he has had to support, and the lack of children to support him when he reaches old age (5–6). Compounded with this, he is now growing older and weaker (7).

Lysias's speech suggests that people who received the dole were not eligible to serve as archon (13). The defendant, in a calculated fit of frustrated sarcasm, says that if his pension is voted away, then he would be able and therefore eligible to serve as archon. It is important to note, though, that the speech does not suggest that men with physical impairments were ineligible to serve as archon. It only suggests that men—with or without physical impairments—who were unable to support themselves and classified among the unable (*adunatoi*) were ineligible to serve as archon. As discussed earlier, blemished men may have been restricted from holding religious office, but what constituted a blemish, and the extent to which the restriction was practiced, are far from clear. After all, lack of wealth would have been a far greater deterrent to holding this office than possession of a limp.[6]

Physical impairment did not in itself evoke pity or admiration. Throughout the speech, the defendant never solicits pity for his impairment, even though an appeal to one's misfortunes was an acceptable courtroom tactic.[7] There was no assumed pity or awe involved in the Greek concept of physical impairment because there were no blanket assumptions about what handicapped people could or could not do, should or should not do.

A physical impairment *in itself* did not constitute a need for money.[8] It is quite possible that some handicapped people begged for their living, but there is no indication that begging was the monopoly of disabled people. There are important differences between the modern and ancient notions of begging. There is a distinction in modern thought between legitimate, handicapped beggars and impostors who mimic a missing leg or a limp.[9] This distinction rests on the assumption that a physical handicap in itself signifies helplessness and merits alms, a notion that was foreign to the Greeks.[10]

Lysias's speech demonstrates that one could be "unable in body" yet not in need of a pension. Xenophon provides another example of physically disadvantaged people who did not need financial help when he suggests that the money for cavalry should come from, among other parties, wealthy men who are "unable in body" (*Cavalry Commander* 9.5–6).

The pension in question in Lysias 24 is not a "pension for the handicapped," a prototype or antecedent of any modern system of disability compensation. If it were, the case would have been about proving that the defendant is genuinely handicapped. That is not an issue. He is. The accuser charges that the defendant rides horses. This charge does not imply that the defendant is faking or exaggerating his handicap while he is actually well enough to mount and ride a horse.[11] Rather, it implies that he is able to make a living so rich that he can afford horses rather than the common transportation for people unable to walk: that ancient equivalent of the wheelchair, the donkey.

The nature and severity of the defendant's physical impairment are not the issue in Lysias 24; the issue is his ability to make a living. The criteria of physical ability and disability rested not on one's ability to function as an individual but on one's functional ability within the community. The question addressed in Lysias 24 is to what extent the defendant is able to function within the community. The accuser charges that he functions very well indeed. In spite of his obvious physical handicap, the defendant may have been voted able-bodied. We do not know the results of the trial.

The dangers of reading the term "*adunatos*" as "disabled," with all its modern social and political connotations, provide an opportunity to summarize three interrelated points that I have made in previous chapters. First, it is not possible to determine any one set of attitudes toward people with disabilities because the notion of physical disability as a classification was foreign to the Greeks. There was no dichotomy of ability and disability; rather, there was a range of conditions to which the human body was always susceptible. In contemporary disability studies, the "medical model" refers to the process by which people are deemed inherently able-bodied or disabled according to medical definition and categorization. By extension, the medical model also refers to the perception of disabilities as permanent illnesses and of disabled people as in perpetual need of medical attention. Physical disability today is an institutionalized phenomenon: in present-day thought, physically disabled people constitute a fairly distinct category with medical parameters. One is pronounced officially "physically disabled" by a medical doctor.

Second, a set of expectations accompanies people with physical disabilities in the modern world. A man who loses his arm in an industrial accident, for example, is not usually expected to heal up and get back to the job. In ancient Greece, we see very few instances in which people with disabilities were banned a priori from certain roles. Completely blind men could not serve in the front lines of the army, and prelingually deaf people, because of the misunderstanding that they were stupid, would not have been eligible for political careers. These were not codified restrictions; only a modern perspective would see this collection of practical circumstances as a set of restrictions related to disability. From the modern perspective, some expectations about disability are codified to the extent that people with some physical disabilities are banned a priori from certain roles: notoriously, in World War II, flat feet were enough to keep men from participating in active duty.

The third implication of physical disability in the modern, developed world that must not be assumed of ancient communities is that physical disability can evoke pity and condescension; the Telethon with its poster child provides an example. Physical disability can also evoke the flip side of pity, awe, moving some to admire accomplishments out of proportion based on the disability, what the disability community calls the supercrip phenomenon. In the ancient Greek world, people with a wide variety of disabilities participated in a wide variety of social, economic, and military roles. People with even the most severe disabilities were integrated into communities that accommodated all ranges of ability. For example, there were military roles for men who could not walk at all, and while congenitally deaf people were considered impaired intellectually, intellectual impairment was not the disaster that the surviving literature suggests.

It is difficult to avoid using golden-age societies as mirrors for our own society and to avoid weighing their historical record on our scales.

Yet in many cases, this has happened in terms of disability in the Classical Greek world. Stripped of the aesthetic, economic, religious, and medical assumptions about disability that we have in the modern world, the picture that emerges of disability in Greek society is perhaps disappointing. In terms of disability, the Greeks were not especially cruel or noble, not especially primitive or advanced. The integration of people with disabilities into Greek communities was not an early form of humanitarian thought, legal accommodation, or enlightened charity. Rather, the Greeks did not waste manpower.

Notes ∾

INTRODUCTION

1. Diana Aitchison, "Medical Miracles Raise Questions about the Value of Life, the Cost of Care," *St. Louis Post Dispatch*, 13 January 2001, A1+.

2. Aitchison, "Medical Miracles," A14.

3. Karen Hagrup [Hirsch], "Culture and Disability: The Role of Oral History," *Oral History Review* 22 (1995): 3.

4. Marion Hathway, *The Young Cripple and His Job* (Chicago: University of Chicago Press, 1928), 66.

5. Joseph P. Shapiro, *No Pity: People with Disabilities Forging a New Civil Rights Movement* (New York: Random House, 1993), 16.

6. For example, see Judith Abrams, *Judaism and Disability: Portrayals in Ancient Texts from the Tanach through the Bavli* (Washington, D.C.: Gallaudet University Press, 1998).

7. J. Lawrence Angel, "Ancient Greek Skeletal Change," *American Journal of Physical Anthropology* 4 (1946): 69–97.

8. Veronique Dasen, *Dwarfs in Ancient Egypt and Greece* (Oxford: Clarendon Press, 1993).

9. Robert Garland, *The Eye of the Beholder: Deformity and Disability in the Graeco-Roman World* (Ithaca: Cornell University Press, 1995).

10. Daniel Ogden, *The Crooked Kings of Ancient Greece* (London: Duckworth, 1997).

11. *Arethusa* 31, no. 3 (fall 1998); James Porter, ed., *Constructions of the Classical Body* (Ann Arbor: University of Michigan Press, 1999).

12. For example, see Nicholas Vlahogiannis's review of *Dwarfs in Ancient Egypt and Greece*, by Veronique Dasen, in *Medical History* 39 (1995): 119–20, for an assessment of the success of Dasen's approach. While I admire Robert Garland's *Eye of the Beholder* as a pioneering work, see my review, *Disability Studies Quarterly* 16 (spring 1996): 36–37, for a critique of the work in terms of disability studies.

13. Oswei Temkin, *The Falling Sickness: A History of Epilepsy from the Greeks to*

the Beginnings of Modern Neurology (Baltimore: Johns Hopkins University Press, 1971).

14. See Robert Garland's excellent article, "Countdown to the Beginning of Time-Keeping," *History Today* 49 (April 1999): 36–42.

CHAPTER ONE

1. Johann Joachim Winckelmann, "On the Imitation of the Painting and Sculpture of the Greeks" (1755), in *Winckelmann: Writings on Art,* ed. David Irwin (London: Phaidon, 1972), 62. Winckelmann goes on (63) to state that "those diseases which are destructive of beauty, were moreover unknown to the Greeks."

2. Raphael, *School of Athens,* 1510. Fresco in the Stanza della Segnatura, Palazzi Vaticani, Vatican State. Reproduced with permission of Scala/Art Resource.

3. Heinrich von Staden, "Incurability and Hopelessness: The *Hippocratic Corpus,*" in *La maladie et les maladies dans la Collection hippocratique,* ed. P. Potter, G. Maloney, and J. Desautels (City of Québec: Les Éditions du Sphinx, 1990), 110–11, concludes that "going on record in a more or less public way with an accurate prognostication of incurability enhances the ancient healer's standing, paradoxically at the very moment when the pronouncement itself unveils the limits of his powers."

4. Edwin Rosner, "Terminologische Hinweise auf die Herkunft der frühen griechischen Medizin," in *Medizingeschichte in unserer Zeit,* ed. H. Eulner et al. (Stuttgart: Ferdinand Enke, 1971), 1–22, catalogs early Greek medical terms and finds (15–16) a preponderance of terms for visible physical characteristics such as rashes and deformities, especially of the trunk and limbs, for which he finds thirty-two terms.

5. Plato may have been referring to the mimes' actors, who were associated with physical deformity, as discussed by Gisela M. A. Richter, "Grotesques and the Mime," *American Journal of Archaeology* 17 (1913): 151–52.

6. Mirko Grmek, *Diseases in the Ancient Greek World,* trans. M. Muellner (Baltimore: Johns Hopkins University Press, 1989), 193, finds that tuberculosis was a common disease during the Classical, Hellenistic, and Roman periods.

7. Homer, *Odyssey,* trans. A. T. Murray (1919; reprint, Cambridge: Harvard University Press, 1984), 1:281.

8. Discussed by Aline Rousselle, *Porneia: On Desire and the Body in Antiquity: Family, Sexuality and Social Relations in Past Times,* trans. F. Pheasant (New York: Oxford University Press, 1988), 5.

9. While there is not enough skeletal evidence to determine any details about the realities of life for people with physical deformity, what evidence there is can simply confirm the existence of some conditions in the ancient world. N-G. Gejvall and F. Henschen, "Two Late Roman Skeletons with Malformation and Close Family Relationship from Ancient Corinth," *Opuscula Atheniensia* 8 (1968): 79–193, report two adult skeletons, one male and one female, both with serious congenital spinal malformation. Robert P. Charles, "Étude anthropologique des nécropoles d'Argos," *Bulletin de correspondance hellénique* 82 (1958): 80, reports a case of congenital dislocation of the hip.

Clubfoot is discussed in some detail by a Hippocratic writer (*On Joints* 62). Galen (18a.668–69) also discusses congenital clubfoot. There is paleopathologic evidence for the existence of the condition in the ancient world. J. Lawrence Angel, *The People of Lerna: Analysis of a Prehistoric Aegean Population* (Princeton: American School of Classical Studies at Athens; Washington, D.C.: Smithsonian Institution Press, 1971), 92, reports the skeleton of a subadult boy with clubfoot from the Middle Bronze Age. The etiology of clubfoot is unknown. George Simons, "Etiological Theories of CTEV," in *The Clubfoot: The Present and a View of the Future*, ed. George Simons (New York: Springer, 1994), 2, summarizes six theories.

10. See the Web site "Orthopedic Topics: Clubfoot," available at <http://www.orthoseek.com/articles/clubfoot.html> accessed 21 November 2002.

11. Mark Golden, "Demography and the Exposure of Girls at Athens," *Phoenix* 35 (1981): 326, n. 37, assembles the evidence that Greek women were fed less well than men were. Patricia E. Levi, "Principles and Mechanisms of Teratogenesis," in *Teratogens: Chemicals Which Cause Birth Defects,* 2d ed., ed. Vera Kolb (Amsterdam: Elsevier, 1993), 7, discusses the teratogenic results of deficiencies, especially of vitamins and minerals.

12. Similarly, Aristotle observes (*History of Animals* 582 b) that if menstruation continues throughout pregnancy, the offspring of such a pregnancy is weak if it even survives.

13. Lesley Dean-Jones, *Women's Bodies in Classical Greek Science* (Oxford: Oxford University Press, 1994), 209–11, discusses the Greek scientific understanding of length of gestation.

14. Mary Ellen Avery and Georgia Littwack, *Born Early* (Boston: Little, Brown, and Company, 1983), 18–19, summarize the possible effects on the fetus of a premature birth.

15. *SEG* 27.1115. Amor López Jimeno and Jesús Nieto Ibáñez, "Nueva Lectura de una *Defixio* de Selinunte (*SEG* XXVII 1115)," *Emerita* 57 (1989): 325–27, discuss the defixio.

16. Margaret M. Hardie, "The Evil Eye in Some Greek Villages of the Upper Haliakmon Valley in West Macedonia," in *The Evil Eye: A Folklore Casebook*, ed. A. Dundes (New York: Garland Publishing, 1981), 107. See also Regina Dionisopolous-Mass, "The Evil Eye and Bewitchment in a Peasant Village," in *The Evil Eye*, ed. C. Maloney (New York: Columbia University Press, 1976), 42–62, for an account of preventive measures and cures for harm done by the evil eye.

17. Pierre Bettez Gravel, *The Malevolent Eye: An Essay on the Evil Eye, Fertility and the Concept of Mana* (New York: Peter Lang, 1995), 12–14.

18. J. Lawrence Angel, "Ancient Skeletons from Asine," in *General Stratigraphical Analysis and Architectural Remains: Asine II: Results of the Excavations East of the Acropolis, 1970–1974*, ed. S. Dietz (Stockholm: Paul Aströms, 1982), 109.

19. Apollodorus 1.3.5; Lucian *On Sacrifices* 6. The chain of events is less clear in the Homeric version (*Iliad* 1.590–94, 18.395–97), where Hephaestus implies that he was hurled to earth because of his lameness. In any case, the fall and the injury are closely connected.

20. Fridolf Kudlien, *Der Beginn des medizinischen Denkens bei den Griechen von Homer bis Hippocrates* (Zurich: Artemis, 1967), 25–26.

21. Ludwig Edelstein and Emma Edelstein, *Asclepius: A Collection and Interpretation of the Testimonies*, 2 vols. (Baltimore: Johns Hopkins University Press,

1945), have collected and translated much of *IG* IV².951, a stele from the healing site at Epidaurus, both sides of which consist of narrations of various complications and cures. Hereafter, I shall refer to the translations of these inscriptions as *ACIT*. The inscription regarding Cephesias: *ACIT* 236.

22. Guido Majno, *The Healing Hand: Man and Wound in the Ancient World* (Cambridge: Harvard University Press, 1975), 188–89, discusses dangerous ancient medical practices in general. See also Lawrence Bliquez, "Greek and Roman Medicine," *Archaeology* 34, no. 2 (1981): 10–17.

23. Actually, Donald Ortner and Walter G. J. Putschar, *Identification of Pathological Conditions in Human Skeletal Remains* (Washington, D.C.: Smithsonian Institution Press, 1985), 63, estimate six weeks, in ideal conditions, for the primary callus to develop.

24. Paul Janssens, *Paleopathology: Diseases and Injuries of Prehistoric Man*, trans. Ida Dequeecker (London: John Baker, 1970), 34.

25. As discussed by Christine F. Salazar, *The Treatment of War Wounds in Graeco-Roman Antiquity* (Leiden: E. J. Brill, 2000), 34–36.

26. Srboljub Živanović, *Ancient Diseases: The Elements of Paleopathology*, trans. L. Edwards (New York: Pica Press, 1982), 171–72. René Bridler, "Das Trauma in der Kunst der griechischen Antike" (Ph.D. diss., Universität Zürich, 1990), 50–86, catalogs the artistic representations from the seventh through the fifth centuries B.C. of injuries inflicted during war. Majno, *The Healing Hand*, 142–47, discusses war wounds, as does Victor Hanson, *The Western Way of War: Infantry Battle in Classical Greece* (New York: Alfred Knopf, 1989), 210–18.

27. A female skeleton from the Byzantine period, for example, shows signs of infection at the site of a fibula fracture. See William Wade, "The Burials," in *Excavations at Nichoria in Southwest Greece*, vol. 3, ed. W. A. McDonald, W. D. E. Coulson, and J. Rosser (Minneapolis: University of Minnesota Press, 1983), 403.

28. As discussed by Nancy Worman, "The Ethics of Style in Sophocles' *Philoctetes*" (paper presented at the annual meeting of the American Philological Association, Atlanta, Ga., 30 December 1994).

29. *Philoctetes*, trans. Kathleen Freeman, in *Ten Greek Plays in Contemporary Translation*, ed. L. R. Lind (Boston: Houghton Mifflin, 1957), 161.

30. Živanović, *Ancient Diseases*, 177–78.

31. Živanović, *Ancient Diseases*, 128, discusses gangrene in the ancient world.

32. Galen 7.80–81, 8.394 describes the symptoms of diabetes in terms of a urinary complication rather than as a metabolic disorder. Also see Grmek, *Diseases in the Ancient Greek World*, 12.

33. Hans Killian, *Cold and Frost Injuries: Rewarming Damages: Biological, Angiological and Clinical Aspects* (Berlin: Springer, 1981), 35, 72, 220–21.

34. Note the striking similarity to Mark 9:43–47.

35. Majno, *The Healing Hand*, 328.

36. Clement J. Michel, "Osteoarthritis," *Primary Care* 20 (December 1993): 815.

37. Angel, "Ancient Skeletons from Asine," 109.

38. J. Lawrence Angel, "Skeletal Material from Attica," *Hesperia* 14 (1945): 297, 300, 303, 305–6, 311. In "Geometric Athenians," in *Late Geometric Graves and a Well in the Agora*, ed. S. Young (*Hesperia*, suppl. 2; Athens: The American

School of Classical Studies at Athens, 1939), Angel notes a young adult male with mild arthritis in the lumbar vertebrae.

39. For current statistics, see Terence W. Starz and Edward B. Miller, "Diagnosis and Treatment of Rheumatoid Arthritis," *Primary Care* 20 (December 1993): 827. For the ancient world, see Živanović, *Ancient Diseases*, 149–51.

40. Simon Byl, "Rheumatism and Gout in the *Corpus Hippocraticum*," *L'Antiquité classique* 57 (1988), 89–102.

41. Angel, "Ancient Skeletons from Asine," 109.

42. For example, Hans D. Betz, *The Greek Magical Papyri in Translation* (Chicago: University of Chicago Press, 1986), 243–44, has assembled several magical preparations and incantations for gouty feet.

43. Živanović, *Ancient Diseases*, 143–44.

44. Of course, medical interpretation of a written sketch is extremely subjective. Garland, *Eye of the Beholder*, 21, reasonably reads this passage as describing the effects of malnutrition.

45. *ACIT* 233. Another account on the reverse side of the stele, *ACIT* 237, describes a man with some sort of foot ailment that Edelstein translates as "gout." Byl, "Rheumatism and Gout," 95, points out that the Greek term referred to any number of conditions, including gout, not all of which would be called gout today.

46. David Morens and Robert Littman, "Epidemiology of the Plague of Athens," *Transactions and Proceedings of the American Philological Association* 122 (1992): 271.

47. Samuel Kottek, *Medicine and Hygiene in the Works of Flavius Josephus* (Leiden: E. J. Brill, 1994), 150–60, catalogs literary records of plague from Thucydides through Josephus.

48. William Stead and Asim K. Dutt, "Epidemiology and Risk Factors," in *Tuberculosis*, ed. D. Schlossberg, 3d ed. (New York: Springer, 1994), 1, report that today, even with the understanding of prevention, including vaccination, there are twenty million active cases worldwide.

49. Živanović, *Ancient Diseases*, 226–29; Janssens, *Paleopathology*, 98; Grmek, *Diseases in the Ancient Greek World*, 183–92.

50. Paul T. Davidson and Enrique Fernandez, "Bone and Joint Tuberculosis," in *Tuberculosis*, ed. D. Schlossberg, 3d ed. (New York: Springer, 1994), 175.

51. The head is determined by Temple Fay et al., "The Head: A Neurosurgeon's Analysis of a Great Stone Portrait," *Expedition* 1, no. 4 (1958–59): 12–18, to represent a man with cerebral palsy. Fay et al. argue (17) that the artist was excellent in detail portrayal and that the head intentionally represents actual asymmetry rather than lack of the sculptor's skill. Even a novice sculptor, they argue, would be able to create a symmetrical pair of lips. Grmek, *Diseases in the Ancient Greek World*, 67–68, notes the need for extreme caution in proposing such clinical interpretations, pointing out that asymmetry in Greek statues from the fifth through third centuries B.C. is common.

52. William Pryse-Phillips, "The Epidemiology of Multiple Sclerosis," in *Handbook of Multiple Sclerosis*, ed. S. Cook (New York: Marcel Dekker, 1990), 2, discusses the north-south gradient of prevalence of multiple sclerosis. The medium-prevalence area in which Greece is included is between thirty-two and forty-seven degrees north.

53. Grmek, *Diseases in the Ancient Greek World,* 75, mentions that only rickets, osteomalacia (softened bones from lack of vitamin D or calcium), and scurvy (which results from forms of vitamin D and vitamin C deficiency) affect the bone system. Don Brothwell and Patricia Brothwell, *Food in Antiquity: A Survey of the Diet of Early Peoples* (London: Thames and Hudson, 1969), 175–92, discuss diet and disease.

54. Peter Garnsey, *Food and Society in Classical Antiquity* (Cambridge: Cambridge University Press, 1999), 47–48.

55. Paul Todd Makler, "New Information on Nutrition in Ancient Greece," *Klio* 62 (1980): 317–19.

56. Garnsey, *Food and Society in Classical Antiquity,* 48.

57. Garnsey, *Food and Society in Classical Antiquity,* 52–53.

58. Regarding cancer, see Spyros Retsas, "On the Antiquity of Cancer: From Hippocrates to Galen," in *Paleo-Oncology: The Antiquity of Cancer,* ed. Spyros Retsas (London: Farrand, 1986), 41–58. Retsas argues (43) that the Hippocratic term "*karkinos*" describes the modern disease with the same clinical name.

G. Bräuer and R. Fricke, "Zur Phänomenologie osteoporotischer Veränderungen bei Bestehen systemischen hämatologischer Affektionen," *Homo* 31 (1980): 198–211, report a case of deformation in the vertebrae in a skeleton at Tiryns, ca. 900–700 B.C., that Grmek, *Diseases in the Ancient Greek World,* 70, interprets as spina bifida.

Grmek (86, 336–37) cites some evidence for the existence of poliomyelitis in the ancient Mediterranean basin but cannot draw sure conclusions.

59. The number of years that constituted old age was probably not parallel to the modern definition, of course. Moses I. Finley, "The Elderly in Classical Antiquity," *Greece and Rome* 28, no. 2 (October 1981): 157, points out that the percentage of the elderly (sixty years or older) in antiquity was much lower than today's figure.

60. Homer, *Iliad,* trans. Richmond Lattimore (Chicago: University of Chicago Press, 1976), x.

61. Aristophanes, trans. B. B. Rogers (1924; reprint, Cambridge: Harvard University Press, 1967), 1:25.

62. The same verb is used by Sophocles when the chorus describes the ever-circling motions of the plough in the field (*Antigone* 340).

63. *Hephaestus' Return,* first quarter of the sixth century B.C., Corinth. National Archaeological Museum, Athens. Cat. number 664 (CC 628). Reproduced with permission from the National Archaeological Museum, Athens. Volume 4, parts 1 and 2, of the *Lexicon Iconographicum Mythologiae Classicae* (*LIMC*) (Zurich: Artemis, 1988) catalogs all known artistic imagery of Hephaestus 1.627–55, 2.386–405. This image is number 129 in part 2. Axel Seeberg, "Hephaistos Rides Again," *Journal of Hellenic Studies* 85 (1965): 103–4, catalogs the four Corinthian vase paintings that depict a sequence in the narrative of Hephaestus's return to Mount Olympus, in which he is seated on a mule in all cases.

64. The Mimnermus fragment is in M. L. West, ed., *Iambi et Elegi Graeci,* 2d ed., 2 vols. (Oxford: Clarendon Press), 1989. Jeffrey Henderson, *The Maculate Muse: Obscene Language in Attic Comedy,* 2d ed. (New York: Oxford University Press, 1991), 154, 157, catalogs the verb (*oiphein*) as a Doric word meaning "to

mount," used only of human beings and used as a euphemistic—not coarse—term for sexual congress in comedy. "The knock-kneed are lustful" may be connected to this proverb, but without context the subtleties are lost (Pseudo-Aristotle *Physiognomics* 810 a). Another proverb associated with mobility impairment, but whose full flavor is lost to us, is seen in Plutarch: "If you live with a lame man you will learn to limp" (*Moralia* 3.6 a).

65. This is repeated in Porphyry frag. 8.10, in J. Bidez, *Vie de Porphye le philosophe néo-platonicien* (Hildesheim: George Olds, 1964).

66. As detailed by Yeongchi Wu and Preston Flanigan, "Rehabilitation of the Lower Extremity Amputee," in *Gangrene and Severe Ischemia of the Lower Extremities,* ed. J. Bergan and J. T. Yao (New York: Grune and Stratton, 1978), 436–37.

67. Athenaeus tells a nearly identical story (8.338 a).

68. Lawrence Bliquez, "Classical Prosthetics," *Archaeology* 36, no. 5 (Sept./Oct. 1983): 29, suggests that if craftsmen, not physicians, created artificial parts, this would explain their absence in medical writings.

69. Plutarch repeats this story of Hegesistratus (*Moralia* 479 b).

70. As explained in Carol Stube Hammersley, "Prosthetic Prescription," in *Lower Extremity Amputation,* ed. Linda A. Karacoloff, Carol Stube Hammersley, and Frederick J. Schneider, 2d ed. (Gaithersburg, Md.: Aspen Publishing, 1992), 59–65. For the disposal of such devices, see Wu and Flanigan, "Rehabilitation of the Lower Extremity Amputee," 437.

71. Linda A. Karacoloff, Carol Stube Hammersley, and Frederick J. Schneider, *Lower Extremity Amputation,* 2d ed. (Gaithersburg, Md.: Aspen Publishing, 1992), 168–74.

72. Bliquez, "Classical Prosthetics," 29, writes that it is not clear how functional this leg would have been: its owner may have walked with a cane or crutch.

73. Bliquez, "Classical Prosthetics," 25. A red-figure vase from southern Italy from the second century B.C. shows a comic figure wearing what at first looks like an artificial leg, but it would be an impossible device to use, as depicted.

74. This maintenance for handicapped war veterans that Plutarch mentions probably represents the origins of the Classical Athenian pension for those unable to fend for themselves, discussed in this book's conclusion. P. J. Rhodes, *A Commentary on the Aristotelian* Athenaion Politeia (Oxford: Clarendon Press, 1981), 570, assembles the evidence for the amount of the dole and points out that the pension was barely sufficient, less than what an unskilled laborer would earn. Arthur Robinson Hands, *Charities and Social Aid in Greece and Rome* (London: Thames and Hudson, 1968), 17–18, discusses the difference between charities as institutions that exist in their own right and the charity of the Classical city-state, which had no legal personality and which was a matter of individual arrangements. Hands finds it unlikely that medical services were ever provided by the state, pointing out that the root of this speculation consists of the testimony of a scholiast to one line of Classical comedy (133–34).

75. Garland, *Eye of the Beholder,* 36. Garland points out that while the very rich might have had a staff of slaves, this would have been the exception (30).

76. This is testimony that Isocrates hopes will win his client's case and so is probably exaggerated, but exaggeration is often the nature of complaint.

CHAPTER TWO

1. This chapter is a heavily modified version of "'Let There Be a Law That No Deformed Child Shall Be Reared': The Cultural Context of Deformity in the Ancient Greek World," *Ancient History Bulletin* 10 (July 1997): 79–92; and "Women and Physical Disability in Ancient Greece," *Ancient World* 29, no. 1 (1998): 3–9.

2. For a discussion of the Greek terms that are often translated as "infanticide" and "exposure," see Mark Golden's endnote to "Demography and the Exposure of Girls at Athens," *Phoenix* 35 (1981): 330–31.

For the conflation of disposal and anomalies, see, for example, Darrel W. Amundsen, "Medicine and the Birth of Defective Children: Approaches of the Ancient World," in *Euthanasia and the Newborn: Conflicts Regarding Saving Lives,* ed. R. McMillan et al. (Dordrecht: D. Reidl Publishing Company, 1987), 10, 13; Paul Carrick, *Medical Ethics in Antiquity: Philosophical Perspectives on Abortion and Euthanasia* (Dordrecht: D. Reidl Publishing Company, 1985), 102; Emeil Eyben, "Family Planning in Graeco-Roman Antiquity," *Ancient Society* 11–12 (1980–81): 15, 35; William L. Langer, "Infanticide: A Historical Survey," *History of Childhood Quarterly* 1, no. 3 (Winter 1974): 353–54.

Helga Kuhse and Peter Singer, *Should the Baby Live? The Problem of Handicapped Infants* (New York: Oxford University Press, 1985), 111, write that infanticide was common among the Greeks and Romans and that the recommendations of the philosophers to destroy defective infants "would not have seemed anything out of the ordinary to their contemporaries." Susan C. M. Scrimshaw, "Infanticide in Human Populations: Societal and Individual Concerns," in *Infanticide: Comparative and Evolutionary Perspectives,* ed. Glenn Haufater and Sarah Blaffer Hrdy (New York: Aldine Publishing Company, 1984), 439, also concludes that "the ancient Greeks destroyed weak, deformed, or unwanted children." In a 1920 essay that argues *against* the probable exposure of infants at Athens, La Rue van Hook accepts as standard practice "the well-known Spartan code" in "The Exposure of Infants at Athens," *Transactions and Proceedings of the American Philological Association* 41 (1920): 143. The on-line encyclopedia *Encarta* (available at <http://encarta.msn.com/find/Concise>; accessed January 2001) states under "Ancient Sparta" that "no deformed child was allowed to live."

3. "Where Helen and Alexander Stopped," available at <http://www.wsu .edu:8080/~dee/GREECE/SPARTA.HTM>, accessed July 1999.

4. Robert F. Weir, *Selective Nontreatment of Handicapped Newborns: Moral Dilemmas in Neonatal Medicine* (New York: Oxford University Press, 1984), 7.

5. The secondary literature on infanticide in Greece is traced and discussed by Ruth Oldenziel, "The Historiography of Infanticide in Antiquity: A Literature Stillborn," in *Sexual Asymmetry: Studies in Ancient Society,* ed. Josine Blok and Peter Mason (Amsterdam: J. C. Gieben, 1987), 87–107. The literature is also summarized by John Boswell, *The Kindness of Strangers: The Abandonment of Children in Western Europe from Late Antiquity to the Renaissance* (New York: Pantheon, 1988), 40–41, n. 96.

6. Cynthia Patterson, "'Not Worth the Rearing': The Causes of Infant Exposure in Ancient Greece," *Transactions of the American Philological Association* 115 (1985): 113–14.

7. Garland, *Eye of the Beholder,* 13–16.

8. Garland, *Eye of the Beholder,* 15.

9. Marc Huys, "The Spartan Practice of Selective Infanticide and Its Parallels in Ancient Utopian Tradition," *Ancient Society* 27 (1996): 47–74.

10. Oldenziel, "The Historiography of Infanticide in Antiquity," 100.

11. Throughout this chapter, I use unpalatable words such as "malformed" and "deformed" to reflect both the modern medical literature and the Greek description of people with physical variations. Such words are unacceptable as colloquial descriptive terms for people, yet it would be artificial and misleading to use a different set of terms when discussing modern medical manuals with "malformed" in the titles. It would also be misleading to disguise the Greek vocabulary in politically correct language. As I point out, the Greeks did, in fact, notice and sometimes deride physical difference, and this is one of the keys to understanding the cultural context into which a physically different child was born.

12. Such questions are indeed worthy of consideration. Mildred Dickemann, "Concepts and Classification in the Study of Human Infanticide: Sectional Introduction and Some Cautionary Notes," in *Infanticide: Comparative and Evolutionary Perspectives,* ed. Glenn Haufater and Sarah Blaffer Hrdy (New York: Aldine Publishing Company, 1984), 428–34, addresses questions such as what constitutes an infant and the importance of considering socioeconomic status as a relevant variable in an investigation of infanticide. It is argued elsewhere that the practice of exposure in general changed over time, increasing in acceptance and frequency after the fourth century B.C. H. Bolkenstien, for example, in "The Exposure of Children at Athens and the *egxutristriai:* Preliminary Note," *Classical Philology* 27 (1922): 222 and passim, argues that there is no evidence for the common practice of exposure at Athens in the fifth century B.C. Oldenziel, "The Historiography of Infanticide in Antiquity," 93–98, traces the scholarship that argues for changes in frequency over time of infanticide and (93) points out the dangers in further fragmenting already fragmentary evidence.

13. Richard M. Goodman and Robert J. Gorlin, *The Malformed Infant and Child: An Illustrated Guide* (New York: Oxford University Press, 1983).

14. Goodman and Gorlin, *The Malformed Infant and Child,* 124–25, 80–81.

15. Severity is determined by the requirement of medical treatment, according to Levi, "Principles and Mechanisms of Teratogenesis," 8.

16. Garland, *Eye of the Beholder,* 65, notes the lack of a Greek record of anomalous birth.

17. Oldenziel, "The Historiography of Infanticide in Antiquity," 88 and passim, discusses the primary sources.

18. G. van N. Viljoen, "Plato and Aristotle on the Exposure of Infants at Athens," *Acta Classica* 2 (1959): 65, concludes that the "secreting away" does not suggest killing.

19. Amundsen, "Medicine and the Birth of Defective Children," 11, calls the vocabulary "frustratingly imprecise."

20. In developed countries today, the size and shape of an infant's body parts can be measured intricately to determine their appropriateness, as outlined in the appendices of Goodman and Gorlin, *The Malformed Infant and Child,* 429–42. There are, for example, twenty-one considerations for the head and face alone to determine normalcy (429–30).

21. van N. Viljoen, "Plato and Aristotle on the Exposure of Infants at Athens," 63.

22. Patterson, "'Not Worth the Rearing,'" 14.

23. The dangers are illustrated well by the unsuccessful attempt of Donald Engels, "The Problem of Female Infanticide in the Greco-Roman World," *Classical Philology* 75 (1980): 112–20, to argue demographically that there is no indication for widespread female infanticide in Classical Greece. The dangers in misusing the small amount of information to draw such conclusions are outlined in the responses to Engels's piece by Golden, "Demography and the Exposure of Girls at Athens," 316–31, and especially William Harris, "The Theoretical Possibility of Extensive Infanticide in the Graeco-Roman World," *Classical Quarterly* 32, no. 1 (1982): 114–16. Bolkenstein, "The Exposure of Children at Athens," argues (222 and passim) that in fact there is no evidence in the fifth or fourth centuries that points to the common practice of exposure at Athens. This much is true, even if Bolkenstein's reading of the evidence, as Oldenziel, "The Historiography of Infanticide in Antiquity," 92, points out, stems from a defense of Athenian democracy.

24. Amundsen, "Medicine and the Birth of Defective Children," 14–15. This is just one example of a common conclusion.

25. S. Y. Samson, "Historical Views of 'Normalcy'," *Collegium Antropologicum* 16 (1992): 251, writes that "it is the intent of this paper to explore and explain several contemporary philosophies of 'normalcy' and to relate them to the philosophy and psychology of disability" but takes for granted that the "during the Greek period (circa 400 B.C.E.), deformed infants were exposed to the elements to die" (252). Similarly, Venetta Lampropoulou, "The History of Deaf Education in Greece," in *The Deaf Way: Perspectives from the International Conference on Deaf Culture,* ed. Carol Erting et al. (Washington, D.C.: Gallaudet University Press, 1995), 240, apparently so took the truism that deformed babies were always discarded for granted that she does not hesitate to state that deaf infants were included among those "with disabilities" in Sparta and "discarded." D. G. Pritchard, *Education and the Handicapped, 1760–1790* (London: Routledge, 1963), 2, also states that the Athenians "killed outright their deaf infants."

26. Jackson Roush, "Screening for Hearing Loss and Otitis Media: Basic Principles," in *Screening for Hearing Loss and Otitis Media in Children,* ed. Jackson Roush (San Diego: Singular, 2001), 3.

27. Kathleen Stassen Berger, *The Developing Person through Childhood,* 2d ed. (New York: Worth Publishing, 2000), 161.

28. Carrick, *Medical Ethics in Antiquity,* 102, 116; Eyben, "Family Planning in Graeco-Roman Antiquity," 15, 77; Garland, *Eye of the Beholder,* 13.

29. In his superb study, Martin Pernick, *The Black Stork: Eugenics and the Death of "Defective" Babies in American Medicine and Motion Pictures since 1915* (New York: Oxford University Press, 1996), 19–20, mentions the "compulsory system" for exposure of deformed infants in Sparta. In this case, Pernick is supported by Plutarch *Lycurgus* 16; I am simply arguing that Plutarch's single statement has been taken as standard practice.

30. As opposed to Weir's conclusion, *Selective Nontreatment of Handicapped Newborns,* 18–19: "Expecting a normal infant to appear at birth, mothers past and present have recoiled at the sight of infants with physical deformities."

31. Karen Metzler, "If There's Life, Make It Worth Living," in *Infanticide and the Value of Life*, ed. Marvin Kohl (Buffalo: Prometheus Books, 1978), 174.

32. Johannes Renger, "Kranke, Krüppel, Debile: Eine Randgruppe in Alten Orient?" in *Außenseiter und Randgruppen: Beiträge zu einer Sozialgeschichte des Alten Orients*, ed. Volkert Haas (Konstanz: Univ. Verlag Konstanz, 1992), 113.

33. As C. S. Bartsocas, "La Génétique dans l'antiquité grecque," *Journal de génétique humaine* 36, no. 4 (1988): 292, points out. Josef Warkany, "Congenital Malformations in the Past," *Journal of Chronic Disease* 10 (1959): 93, suggests that the lines of Empedocles describing peripatetic, disjointed heads and limbs reflect the existence of "human monstrosities."

34. Robert Étienne, "Ancient Medical Conscience and the Life of Children," trans. Michèle Morris, *Journal of Psychohistory* 4 (1977): 153, finds that no doctor was very interested in infant medicine or in the sickness or wellness of infants and children generally.

35. Pernick, *The Black Stork*, 14, discusses the imposition of standards of normalcy and eugenics on mass culture and (60–65) traces the nineteenth- and twentieth-century construction and fabrication of beauty as a mark of hereditary fitness and deformity as a mark of inferiority, even evil inferiority, and sickness.

36. Discussed by P. Louis, "Monstres et monstruosités dans la Biologie d'Aristote," in *Le Monde Grec: Hommages à Claire Préaux*, ed. J. Bingen, G. Combier, and G. Nachtergal (Brussels: Éditions de l'université de Bruxelles, 1978), 277–84.

37. As outlined by Lennard Davis, *Enforcing Normalcy: Disability, Deafness and the Body* (London: Verso, 1995), 23–49.

38. Davis, *Enforcing Normalcy*, 25.

39. Homer, *Odyssey*, trans. A. T. Murray, 1:281.

40. Harlan Hahn, "Disability and Classical Aesthetic Canons" (N.p., 1993), 20, points out that the Classical sculptors, in using a mathematical ratio to express absolute beauty, set a standard of evaluation of physical beauty to which "generations of Westerners have remained steadfastly wedded." Davis, *Enforcing Normalcy*, 25, argues that in premodern societies the artistic ideal was unattainable, that all people are below the ideal and by default belong to the category of grotesque.

41. Robert P. Charles, "Etude anthropologique des nécropoles d'Argos," *Bulletin de correspondance hellénique* 82 (1958): 275.

42. Euterpe Bazopoulou-Kyrkanidou, "What Makes Hephaestus Lame?" *American Journal of Medical Genetics* 72, no. 2 (1997): 149–51.

43. For example, see Paul Longmore, "Screening Stereotypes: Images of Disabled People," *Social Policy* 16, no. 1 (1985): 31–37. The entire volume of *Disability Studies Quarterly* 15 (1992) was devoted to a summary and discussion of the large body of literature on the portrayal of disability in the media. For more recent information, see also "Mass Media and Disability Links," available at <http://saber.towson.edu/~bhalle/disable.html>, accessed November 21, 2002.

44. I thank D. P. M. Weerakkody for pointing out that Diodorus may be taking a jab at Plato's criteria for membership in a utopian community in this parody of utopian literature. D. P. M. Weerakkody, "Comment on Article," E-mail to the author, 20 September 1999.

45. Curtius Rufus 9.1.24–26 repeats the story. Other reports of such utopias

are discussed in detail by Huys, "The Spartan Practice of Selective Infanticide," 59–74.

46. Maciej Henneberg and Renata Henneberg, "Biological Characteristics of the Population Based on an Analysis of Skeletal Remains," in *The Chora of Metaponto: The Necropoleis*, ed. J. Coleman Carter (Austin: Institute of Classical Archaeology, 1998), 2:527.

47. Pliny *Natural History* 7.1.3 describes the weak and helpless human infant. Mark Golden, *Children and Childhood in Classical Athens* (Baltimore: Johns Hopkins University Press, 1990), 16–17, summarizes the Classical Athenian perception of newborns as smooth and soft, lacking in intelligence and strength, and helpless.

48. Golden, *Children and Childhood in Classical Athens*, 7.

49. *ACIT* 221–37.

50. Garnsey, *Food and Society in Classical Antiquity*, 48, discusses swaddling as a contributing factor to rickets.

51. Clubfoot can, in fact, be eliminated in this way, as discussed by R. Seringe et al., "A New Articulated Splint for Clubfeet," in *The Clubfoot: The Present and a View of the Future*, ed. George Simons (New York: Springer, 1994), 187–90. S. Zimbler, "Nonoperative Management of the Equinovarus Foot: Long-Term Results," in *The Clubfoot*, 192–93, concludes that while only 10 percent of children with clubfeet have a mild enough condition to make nonoperative treatment worthwhile, the patients who are treated nonoperatively are superior, functionally, to those patients whose clubfoot is corrected surgically.

52. Garland, *Eye of the Beholder*, 15. W. K. Lacey, *The Family in Classical Greece* (Ithaca: Cornell University Press, 1968), 164, also supposes that not all babies with deformities were killed, but in support of this point mentions the survival of at least one man with poor eyesight who appears in a speech of Aeschines (1.102–4). As Boswell, *Kindness of Strangers*, 40–41, n. 96., points out, it is not logical to assume that this particular man was born with poor eyesight or that, even if he were, it could be detected. A. W. Gomme, *The Population of Athens in the Fifth and Fourth Centuries B.C.* (1933; reprint, Chicago: Argonaut, 1967), 82, responds to A. Cameron, "The Exposure of Children and Greek Ethics," *The Classical Review* 46 (1932), who implies that by Aristotle's time exposure was an established custom (108–9). Gomme argues that Aristotle (*Politics* 7.16.15) is advocating a new method (i.e., exposure) that had not been carried out before and that he knows will be repugnant to many.

53. Langer, "Infanticide: A Historical Survey," 353–54.

54. Ingomar Weiler, "Soziale Randgruppen in der antiken Welt: Einführung und wissenschaftsgeschichtliche Aspekte: Ausgewählte Literatur zur historichen Randgruppenforschung," in *Soziale Randgruppen und Außenseiter im Alterum*, ed. Ingomar Weiler (Graz: Leykam, 1988), 14.

55. Several disability-studies models are summarized by Beth Haller, "Rethinking Models of Media Representation of Disability," *Disability Studies Quarterly* 15, no. 2 (Spring 1995): 29–30. Simi Linton, in *Claiming Disability: Knowledge and Identity* (New York: New York University Press, 1998), 38–70, traces six models in disability studies.

56. Renger, "Kranke, Krüppel, Debile," 121, points to blind people, for example, as part of society, as they had jobs as millers, grinders, and so on.

57. As Henri-Jacques Stiker, *Corps infirmes et sociétés* (Paris: Aubier Montage, 1982) 59, points out.

58. The editor of this collection of papyri, J. R. Rea, notes that the term suggests "cripple" or "short," but points out that it could also simply be a name.

59. Kassel and Austin, *PCG,* 59, in their commentary on fragment 57, mention a statue of a youth with a deformed foot, a Roman work imitating Hellenistic style, described by Gisela M. A. Richter, *Catalogue of Greek and Roman Antiquities in the Dumbarton Oaks Collection* (Cambridge: Harvard University Press, 1956), 32–35. Richter states (4) that the depiction of the clubfoot is intentional and not sloppy execution of the statue, given the statue's overall excellence.

P. Tebt. 2.323–25, from A.D. 47, records the division of four slaves, one of them the lame Heracles, among three brothers. The youngest brother is given two of the four slaves; of these two, one is to be contracted to the men's mother until her death; the other is the lame Heracles.

60. Alison Burford, *Craftsmen in Greek and Roman Society* (Ithaca: Cornell University Press, 1972), 72.

61. This epithet is seen in Homer *Iliad* 8.371, 20.270, 21.331.

62. Hephaestus, drunk and supported by a satyr. Red-figure pelike, 435–430 B.C. Munich Archaeological Collection. Reproduced with permission from Art Resource.

63. Kurt Aterman, "From Horus the Child to Hephaestus Who Limps: A Romp through History," *The American Journal of Medical Genetics* 83, no. 1 (1999): 63. Aterman argues that depictions of Hephaestus with malformed feet represent another version of the god that is connected with Egyptian gods such as Bes who have characteristics of dwarfism.

64. Paul Stengel, *Die Griechischen Kultusaltertümer* (Munich: C. H. Beck, 1920), 38–39.

65. *SIG* 1009; W. Dittenberger, ed., *Sylloge Inscriptionum Graecarum* (Hildesheim: Georg Olms, 1960), 3:144–45.

The fragment of Attic comedy is in T. Kock, ed., *Comicorum Atticorum Fragmenta* (Leipzig: Teubner, 1884), 2:150.

66. Stengel, *Die Griechischen Kultusaltertümer,* 38.

67. Abrams, *Judaism and Disability,* 16–70, 123, points out that any sort of blemish or physical imperfection would have barred service in the Temple under Hebrew law, even if such people were not banished from everyday life in the Jewish community.

68. W. G. Thalmann, "Thersites: Comedy, Scapegoats, and Heroic Ideology in the *Iliad*," *Transactions and Proceedings of the American Philological Association* 118 (1988): 1.

69. Jan Bremmer, "Scapegoat Rituals in Ancient Greece," in *Oxford Readings in Greek Religion,* ed. R. G. A. Buxton (Oxford: Oxford University Press, 2000), 275–76.

70. As Robert Garland discusses in "The Mockery of the Deformed and Disabled in Graeco-Roman Culture," in *Laughter Down the Centuries,* ed. S. Jäkel and A. Timonen (Turku, Finland: Turun Yliopisto, 1994), 1:71–84.

71. In addition to the description of Thersites' appearance in the *Iliad,* Plutarch *Moralia* 35 c mentions Thersites' humpback.

72. Hanson, *Western Way of War,* 95, points out that in hoplite battle, neither speed nor agility was necessary, but that the crucial quality was determination to stand one's ground, keeping the line intact.

73. Whether Demosthenes portrayed Philip's physical characteristics accurately or not, Plutarch *Moralia* 739 b shows that Philip II was remembered as having a lame leg.

74. Similarly, Aratus was carried on a litter to his campaigns when he put his leg out of joint (Plutarch *Aratus* 33.4, 34.4).

75. Barry Baldwin, "Medical Grounds for Exemptions from Military Service at Athens," *Classical Philology* 62 (1967): 42–43.

76. Dean-Jones, *Women's Bodies in Classical Greek Science,* 41–42, discusses the process by which cultures can develop science to support the belief that men and women are very different from each other.

77. Raphael Sealey, *Women and Law in Classical Greece* (Chapel Hill: University of North Carolina Press, 1990), 14.

78. Herodotus never states explicitly, perhaps because there was no need, that it was Labda's lameness that made her unmarriageable. Garland, *Eye of the Beholder,* 98, states that Labda was not easily marriageable because the lameness may have been unattractive and adds the possibility of the fear that Labda's off-spring would be lame as well.

79. Walter Scheidel, "The Most Silent Women of Greece and Rome: Rural Labor and Women's Life in the Ancient World," part 1, *Greece and Rome* 42, no. 2 (October 1995): 202–17, and part 2, *Greece and Rome* 43, no. 1 (April 1996): 1–10, assembles the scanty source material. Scheidel, "The Most Silent Women," part 2, using source and comparative material, describes the work of the rural woman as consisting of tasks such as tending livestock, harvesting, and threshing.

80. As discussed by Roger Brock, "The Labour of Women in Classical Athens," *Classical Quarterly* 44, no. 2 (1994): 336–46.

81. Scheidel, "The Most Silent Women" part 2, 1, mentions the participation of women in both activities.

82. Carolyn Dewald, "Women and Culture in Herodotus' *Histories,*" in *Reflections of Women in Antiquity,* ed. H. Foley (New York: Gordon and Breach Science Publishers, 1981), 120, catalogs the tale of Labda in the category of "individual passive women presented in a family context" and in the subcategory of "family and difficulties of generation," in which the tale of Labda is one of nine instances.

83. David Schaps, *Economic Rights of Women in Ancient Greece* (Edinburgh: Edinburgh University Press, 1979), 74.

84. Nancy Demand, *Birth, Death, and Motherhood in Classical Greece* (Baltimore: Johns Hopkins University Press, 1994), 17, discusses the importance of producing a child. Of the new bride, she writes that "only the birth of a child gave her full status as a *gyne,* woman-wife. All eyes would therefore be upon her in the early days of marriage."

Sealey, *Women and Law in Classical Greece,* 158, finds that Athenian law assumes that women should bear children.

85. Jean-Nicolas Corvisier, *Santé et société en Grèce ancienne* (Paris: Economica, 1985), 161–62. Corvisier organizes several categories of sterility that appear in the medical texts.

86. Corvisier, *Santé et société en Grèce ancienne,* 121–22, catalogs the thanks for fertility at Epidaurus.

87. Earl R. Carlson, *Born That Way* (New York: John Day, 1941), 5.

88. Golden, *Children and Childhood in Classical Athens,* 17, points out the archaeological evidence for feeding bottles and potty stools.

89. Demand, *Birth, Death, and Motherhood,* 7, discusses sex selection not by conscious intention but by neglect in care and feeding. Garnsey, *Food and Society in Classical Antiquity,* 106, points out that the patterns of care and feeding of children in the Graeco-Roman world were conducive to "early death, stunted development or selective malnutrition."

90. As Patterson, " 'Not Worth the Rearing,' " 114, argues.

91. Lennard Davis, "Dr. Johnson, Ameila, and the Discourse of Disability," in *"Defects": Engendering the Modern Body,* ed. H. Deutsch and F. Nussbaum (Ann Arbor: University of Michigan Press, 2000), 54–74.

92. Huys, "The Spartan Practice of Selective Infanticide," 74.

93. Gail H. Landsman, "Reconstructing Motherhood in the Age of 'Perfect' Babies: Mothers of Infants and Toddlers with Disabilities," *Signs* 24 (autumn 1998): 95. See also Ruth Hubbard, "Abortion and Disability: Who Should and Should Not Inhabit the World?" in *The Disability Studies Reader,* ed. Lennard Davis (New York: Routledge, 1997), 187–200.

CHAPTER THREE

1. "Demosthenes," available at <http://encarta.msn.com/index/conciseindex/6b/06ba7000.htm>, accessed June 1999.

2. See, for example, Walter Manning, *Clinical Decision Making in the Diagnosis and Treatment of Fluency Disorders* (Albany: Delmar Publishers, 1996), 43; Franklin Silverman, *Stuttering and Other Fluency Disorders,* 2d ed. (Boston: Allyn and Bacon, 1996), 7, 11.

3. "Stottervereniging Demosthenes," available at <http://www.stotteren.nl/demosthenes>, accessed November 2000.

4. Margaret Eldridge, *A History of the Treatment of Speech Disorders* (Edinburgh: E. and S. Livingstone, 1968), 6, points out that the Greek vocabulary does not necessarily describe stuttering, only a "speech problem." Charles van Riper, *The Nature of Stuttering,* 2d ed. (Englewood Cliffs, N.J.: Prentice-Hall, 1982), 3, also points this out.

5. Oliver Bloodstein, *A Handbook on Stuttering,* 5th ed. (San Diego: Singular Publishing Group, 1995), 131–43; van Riper, *Nature of Stuttering,* 4–9.

6. A widely cited statistic, provided by, among others, Bloodstein, *Handbook on Stuttering,* 107.

7. Pam Grunwell, "Assessment of Articulation and Phonology," in *Assessment in Speech and Language Therapy,* ed. J. Beech and L. Harding (London: Routledge, 1993), 52–53, lists about a dozen physical factors that can affect speech fluency, including jaw alignment, palatal structure, and the structure of the lips and tongue. As an example of a person with a physical factor that may have affected speech fluency, Angel, "Skeletal Material from Attica," 303, reports the skull of a person with an overbite from the Sub-Mycenaean or early Protogeometric period.

We do not know the degree of the overbite of this person, but a serious overbite can affect speech articulation.

8. A definition and overview of cleft lip and palate and their treatments are provided by Michael Benninger and Glendon Gardner, "Medical and Surgical Management in Otolaryngology," in *Medical Speech-Language Pathology: A Practitioner's Guide*, ed. Alex Johnson and Barbara Jacobson (New York: Theme, 1998), 500–502.

9. Živanović, *Ancient Diseases*. Angel, *People of Lerna*, 90, estimates that during the Classical period, 40 percent of the population had pronounced to very pronounced dental abrasion, some of which must have affected speech.

10. Grunwell, "Assessment of Articulation and Phonology," 52.

11. C. Woodruff Starkweather and Janet Givens-Ackerman, *Stuttering* (Austin: Pro-Ed, 1997), 24.

12. Jannet Wright, "Assessment of Children with Special Needs," in *Assessment in Speech and Language Therapy*, ed. J. Beech and L. Harding (New York: Routledge, 1993), 138, discusses other related issues, such as problems with coordination, that affect nonverbal aspects of communication and further complicate the ability to produce intelligible speech.

13. Jean Kerr, "Assessment of Acquired Language Problems," in *Assessment in Speech and Language Therapy*, ed. J. Beech and L. Harding (New York: Routledge, 1993), 100.

14. Catherine Mateer, "Neural Bases of Language," in *Neuropsychology of Stuttering*, ed. E. Boberg (Edmonton: University of Alberta Press, 1993), 20.

15. Linda Armstrong, "Assessing the Older Communication-Impaired Person," in *Assessment in Speech and Language Therapy*, ed. J. Beech and L. Harding (New York: Routledge, 1993), 166, lists several causes of communication impairment in old age, including stroke, tumor, head injury, and degenerative diseases such as Alzheimer's disease.

16. Lena Rustin and Armin Kuhr, *Social Skills and the Speech Impaired* (London: Taylor and Francis, 1989), 53.

17. This theory of the tightly fastened tongue is repeated by the Roman Pliny the Elder (*Natural History* 11.65.174).

18. Yves Violé O'Neill, *Speech and Speech Disorders in Western Thought before 1600* (Westport, Conn.: Greenwood Press, 1980), 28, summarizes the contributions of the Hippocratic corpus in terms of speech disorders as the recognition that the origin of speech is the head and that an injury to the head can affect speech. A. Souques, *Étapes de la neurologie dans l'antiquité grecque* (Paris: Libraries de L'Académie de Médicine, 1936), 12, 18, 116, considers the Hellenistic period, especially Herophilus, the high point of Greek culture from a neurologist's perspective.

19. As R. W. Reiber and Jeffrey Wollock, "The Historical Roots of the Theory and Therapy of Stuttering," in *The Problem of Stuttering*, ed. R. W. Reiber (New York: Elsevier, 1977), 3–5, point out. Reiber and Wollock suggest that while Galen is more methodical in his use of the terms than the Hippocratic authors, the terms for speech disorders must be understood as symptoms of unbalanced humors rather than as disorders themselves.

20. Ronald Sommers, *Articulation Disorders* (Englewood Cliffs, N.J.: Prentice-Hall, 1983), 2, points out that the analysis of the way that speech is produced is artificial.

21. After the first use of "to stutter" (*battarizein*) by Hipponax (frag. 140 in West, *Iambi et Elegi Graeci*), the term appears only rarely until after the first century A.D.

22. *Prometheus Bound*, trans. Rex Warner, in *Ten Greek Plays in Contemporary Translation*, ed. L. R. Lind (Boston: Houghton Mifflin, 1957), 25–26. Similarly, Aristotle *Metaphysics* 985 a, commenting on Empedocles, refers to ideas expressed unclearly (*psellizetai legôn*), not literally slurred.

23. Mark Golden, "Baby Talk and Child Language in Ancient Greece," in *Lo Spettacolo delle Voci*, ed. Francesco de Martino and Alan. H. Sommerstein (Bari: Levante, 1995), 11–34, concludes that it is difficult to summarize any overall Greek attitudes toward childhood speech.

24. Johannes Tzetzes, *Commentarium In Nubes* 1381 a, commenting on Aristophanes seventeen centuries after he wrote, interprets Pheidippides' lisping (*traulizontos*) as childish little stammering (*nêpios hupopsellizontos*).

25. George Petzl, ed., *Die Inschriften von Smyrna* (Bonn: Rudolf Habelt, 1982), 520.

26. In the first surviving mention of Battus, Pindar *Pythian Odes* 5.58–59 mentions only that lions fled in fear of his tongue. Sandys reasonably translates it as "strange" tongue, although there is actually no "strange" in the Greek text. Pausanias 10.15.6 tells us that Battus's voice was healed when he was terrified at the sight of a lion.

27. Joseph G. Sheehan, *Stuttering: Research and Therapy* (New York: Harper and Row, 1970), 39, comments that stutterers are more prone to stutter in familiar surroundings; thus, the oracle's recommendation that Battus banish himself forever is "a prescription many a modern speech therapist would occasionally like to use." Van Riper, *Nature of Stuttering*, 3, also makes this observation.

28. Bruno Gentili, *Poetry and Its Public in Ancient Greece from Homer to the Fifth Century*, trans. A. Thomas Cole (Baltimore: Johns Hopkins University Press, 1988), 5, citing Plato, reminds us that oral performance is created for the ear. In other words, we have lost the context that may have clarified the vocabulary, and there was probably more than one interpretation of the vocabulary.

29. O. Masson, "Le nom de Battos, fondateur de Cyrene," *Glotta* 54 (1976): 84–98. Masson cites other similar cases of physical disabilities that become proper names, such as the deformity of the foot (*kullos*) and the name Kullaros, the physical characteristic "squinting" (*mullos*) and the name Mullos, and so on. He conjectures the existence of a now-lost older term "stutter" (*battos*).

30. Here, Plutarch echoes Plato (*Laws* 474 d–e), who supposes that any physical characteristic, such as a crooked nose, can be taken as a good sign in one's beloved.

31. Quintilian does not mention this exercise in connection with Demosthenes' voice problems, though this passage has been taken to refer to his speech disorder; see, e.g., Eldridge, *History of the Treatment of Speech Disorders*, 12.

32. Henderson, *Maculate Muse*, 203, lists "*batalos*" as a term for "anus" and concludes, citing Aeschines *On the False Embassy* 99 and Demosthenes *On the Crown* 180, that it was used in mockery of both people who debauched themselves and stammerers.

33. Homer, *Iliad*, trans. Richard Lattimore, 65, 106.

34. Aristotle, *The Nicomachean Ethics*, trans. H. Rackman, vol. 19 (Cambridge: Harvard University Press, 1934).

35. Mary Lefkowitz, *The Lives of the Greek Poets* (Baltimore: Johns Hopkins University Press, 1981), compiles Sophocles' life and evaluates the primary sources (75–87) and includes as appendix 4 the biography "The Life of Sophocles" (160–63). The passages cited in this biography are 1 (Sophocles' participation in government), 3 (his training of boys), and 4 (his weak voice).

36. Danielle Gourevitch, *Le mal d'être femme: La femme et la medecine dans la Rome antique* (Paris: Societe d'edition "Les Belles Lettres," 1984).

37. The persistence of the concept that humors were configured differently in men and in women is illustrated in Zirka Z. Filipczak, *Hot Dry Men, Cold Wet Women: The Theory of Humors in Western European Art, 1575–1700* (New York: The American Federation of Arts, 1997).

38. Dean-Jones, *Women's Bodies in Classical Greek Science*, 57–58.

39. Women were, as Roger Just argues in *Women in Athenian Law and Life* (New York: Routledge, 1989), representatives of nature, not culture; this was codified in Athenian law.

40. Plutarch, *Moralia*, trans. Frank Cole Babbit, in *Plutarch's Moralia*, vol. 5 (1936; reprint, Cambridge: Harvard University Press, 1984).

41. Euripides, *Medea and Other Plays*, trans. Philip Vellacott (New York: Penguin, 1963).

42. As Ellen D. Reeder, "Women and Men in Classical Greece," in *Pandora: Women in Classical Greece*, ed. Ellen D. Reeder (Baltimore: Trustees of the Walters Art Gallery and Princeton University Press, 1995), 26, points out.

43. As discussed by Nancy Sorkin Rabinowitz, "Female Speech and Female Sexuality: Euripides' *Hippolytus* as Model," *Helios* 13, no. 2 (1986): 127–40.

44. As narrated by Robert Bogdan, *Freak Show: Presenting Human Oddities for Amusement and Profit* (Chicago: University of Chicago Press, 1988).

45. Plato's *Menexenus* (235e–236d, 249d–e) is the main source for Aspasia's life.

46. Madeleine Henry, *Prisoner of History: Aspasia of Miletus and Her Biographical Tradition* (New York: Oxford University Press, 1995), 35.

47. Thucydides. Trans. C. Smith (Cambridge, MA: 1919, reprint, Harvard University Press, 1991), 1:341.

48. As Alganza Roldán Minerva argues in "La mujer en la historiografía griega helenística: Polibio, mujeres e historia viril," in *La mujer en el mundo mediterráneo antiguo*, ed. A. López, C. Martínez, and A. Pociña (Granada: Universidad de Granada, 1990): 54–72.

49. Graham Wylie, "Demosthenes the General: Protagonist in a Greek Tragedy?" *Greece and Rome* 40, no. 1 (April 1993): 20–30.

50. See, for example, Larry Gonick, *The Cartoon History of the Universe, Volumes 1–7: From the Big Bang to Alexander the Great* (New York: Doubleday, 1990), 336.

51. "Stuttering Didn't Keep Her Grounded," public service advertisement. Used with permission from the Stuttering Foundation of America, Memphis, Tenn.

52. Linton, *Claiming Disability*, 18.

53. Linton, *Claiming Disability*, 18. See also Shapiro, *No Pity*, 3, who suggests that an equivalent to "I never think of you as disabled" is "You're the least black person I've ever met."

54. The controversy over Christopher Reeve's campaign to cure rather than

accept physical disability is ongoing. Excellent discussions can be found in two essays in *Ragged Edge* 1 (January/February 1997): David Mitchell's "The Frontier That Never Ends" (20–21) and Pat Williams's "Christopher Reeve: What's It Gonna Take?" (16–19).

The emphasis on oral education for deaf children is summarized by Douglas Baynton in *Forbidden Signs: American Culture and the Campaign against Sign Language* (Chicago: University of Chicago Press, 1996).

55. Cheryl Marie Wade's "I Am Not One Of The," the poem from which this line is taken, is widely anthologized, e.g., in *The Disability Studies Reader,* ed. Lennard Davis (New York: Routledge, 1997), 408.

56. Starkweather and Givens-Ackerman, *Stuttering,* 4–5, discuss discrimination against stutterers in relation to the ADA. Also see Rosemarie Garland Thomson, *Extraordinary Bodies: Figuring Physical Disability in American Culture and Literature* (New York: Columbia University Press, 1997), 137.

CHAPTER FOUR

1. The title of this chapter is modeled after Eleftheria Bernidaki-Aldous's *Blindness in a Culture of Light: Especially in the Case of* Oedipus at Colonus *of Sophocles* (New York: Peter Lang, 1990). This chapter is a modified version of "Deaf and Dumb in Ancient Greece," in *The Disability Studies Reader,* ed. Lennard Davis (New York: Routledge, 1997), 29–51.

2. Nanci Scheetz, *Orientation to Deafness* (Boston: Allyn and Bacon, 1993), 203.

3. Majno, *The Healing Hand,* 171–75.

4. Grmek, *Diseases in the Ancient Greek World,* 334–37, sees evidence for chickenpox, the common cold virus, and mumps. He also sees evidence for the possibility of the influenza virus and poliomyelitis. He does not believe that the measles virus existed. Živanović, *Ancient Diseases,* 86, 108, finds possible skeletal evidence for poliomyelitis.

5. Grmek, *Diseases in the Ancient Greek World,* 122, 123, 131, discusses meningitis in ancient Greece.

6. Robert Sallares, *The Ecology of the Ancient Greek World* (Ithaca: Cornell University Press, 1991), 235.

7. Nora Groce, *Everyone Here Spoke Sign Language: Hereditary Deafness on Martha's Vineyard* (Cambridge: Harvard University Press, 1985). Groce discusses inbreeding on this isolated island (40–43).

8. M. Michael Cohen and Robert J. Gorlin, "Epidemiology, Etiology, and Genetic Patterns," in *Hereditary Hearing Loss and Its Syndromes,* ed. Robert J. Gorlin, H. Toriello, and M. Michael Cohen (New York: Oxford University Press, 1995), 9–21, discuss the varieties of genetic deafness in the modern world, listing hereditary factors, acquired factors, and unknown factors as about equal as causes of genetic hearing loss (9). The subcategories of genetic deafness in the ancient world are impossible to determine.

9. J. A. Mason and K. R. Herrmann, "Universal Infant Hearing Screening by Automated Auditory Brainstem Response Measurement," *Pediatrics* 101 (1998): 221–28.

10. Gerhard Salomon, "Hearing Problems and the Elderly," *Danish Medical Bulletin Special Supplement Series on Gerontology* 33 (suppl. 3; 1996): 4.

11. Grmek, *Diseases in the Ancient Greek World*, 103, gives 41.7 years as the average age of adults at the moment of death in Greece during Classical times. Mogens Herman Hansen, *Demography and Democracy: The Number of Athenian Citizens in the Fourth Century B.C.* (Denmark: Systime, 1986), 12, calculates that in the fourth century, of all the males in Attica who were between eighteen and eighty-plus years of age, 11.9 percent were fifty to sixty-nine years old, and 8.7 percent were sixty to eighty years and older.

12. Donna Williams, *Somebody Somewhere: Breaking Free from the World of Autism* (New York: Times Books, 1994), 50.

13. W. Pötscher, "Der stumme Sohn der Kroisos," *Zeitschrift für klinische Psychologie und Psychotherapie* 20 (1974): 368, argues that Croesus's son was not deaf at all, pointing out that, in order to finally speak, he must have been able to hear all along. He suggests that Herodotus used "deaf" as an interchangeable word for "mute."

14. Petzl, *Die Inschriften von Smyrna*, 1, no. 549.

15. Xenophon *Cyropaedia* 7.2.20 repeats the assessment.

16. As mentioned by Sarah Pomeroy, "Infanticide in Hellenistic Greece," in *Images of Women in Antiquity*, ed. A. Cameron and A. Kuhrt, 2d ed. (Detroit: Wayne State University Press, 1993), 208.

17. J. A. S. Evans, *Herodotus: Explorer of the Past* (Princeton: Princeton University Press, 1991), 49.

18. Harlan Lane, *When the Mind Hears: A History of the Deaf* (New York: Random House, 1985), 93, points out that about ten centuries later, deaf people appeared as a legal class for the first time, in the Code of Justinian (3.20.7, 6.22.10).

19. Danielle Gourevitch, "L'Aphonie hippocratique," in *Formes de pensée dans la Collection hippocratique: Actes du IVe Colloque International Hippocratique*, ed. F. Lasserre and P. Mudry (Geneva: Librarie Droz, 1983), 302, points out that muteness (*aphônos*) appears in the Hippocratic corpus as a symptom rather than as a condition in itself and that while the Hippocratics recognized that there were different degrees and types of muteness, the aim of the practitioners was objective reporting, not analysis.

20. This sort of passing deafness is seen especially frequently throughout *Epidemics;* see, for example, 1.3.13(3).5, 15, 16; 1.3.13(5).26; 1.3.13(10).4, and so on. In the writings of Galen, there are twenty-five instances of the term "deaf" (*kôphos*), four in Pseudo-Galen. Of these, almost all are references to the temporary deafness of the Hippocratic corpus; see, for example, 17a.528.5, 17a.530.2, 17a.530.7, 17a.534.4, 17a.557.16, 17a.560.10, 17a.585.7, 17a.587.2.

21. Deafness as a result of a misdirected lochial purge: Hippocrates *On the Conditions of Women* 41.30. Muteness as an accompanying symptom of hysteria: *On the Nature of Women* 23.1; *On the Conditions of Women* 127.1, 201.13, 203.18. Gourevitch, *Le mal d'être femme*, 113–28, provides a good discussion of female hysteria in general.

22. Huldrych Koelbing, *Arzt und Patient in der antiken Welt* (Munich: Artemis, 1977), 158, points out that although Celsus worked during the Roman, not the Hellenistic, period, his work is more a compilation of Hellenistic scientific writing than a reflection of his own practice.

23. Similar examples: *Prorrhetic* 1.127; *Coan Prognosis* 324, 623.

24. In case Celsus's treatment seems quaint, I should note Lane's work *When the Mind Hears,* the first part of which is written as an autobiography of Laurent Clerc, a nineteenth-century deaf man who submitted to visits to a doctor who injected mysterious liquids into his ears in an attempt to cure his deafness (5). Galen (10.358) includes an ear syringe in his list of physicians' tools such as catheters and syringes.

25. Garland, *Eye of the Beholder,* 96–97, sees Croesus's son's spontaneous recovery as a symbol that the son was, after all, worthwhile and that Croesus's moral blindness toward his son is parallel with his senseless invasion of Persia. Pötscher, "Der stumme Sohn der Kroisos," 367–68, argues that the muteness was psychogenic and not connected with deafness at all.

26. Mabel Lang, *Cure and Cult in Ancient Corinth: A Guide to the Asklepion* (Princeton: American School of Classical Studies at Athens, 1977), 15, uses headache as an example of an abstract ailment.

27. F. T. van Straten, "Gifts for the Gods," in *Faith, Hope and Worship,* ed. H. S. Versnel (Leiden: E. J. Brill, 1981), 105–43, catalogs votive offerings representing body parts from the Greek world. Models of ears were found on many sites.

28. Van Straten, "Gifts for the Gods," 110, points out that while there are no surviving examples of mouths, there is testimony for eight examples at the Athenian Asclepion.

29. H. S. Versnel, "Religious Mentality in Ancient Prayer," in *Faith, Hope and Worship,* ed. H. S. Versnel (Leiden: E. J. Brill, 1981), 30.

30. Van Straten, "Gifts for the Gods," 83. Van Straten points out (144) that he restricted the ears, in his catalog of body parts, to the ears that were votive offerings, not representations of gods' ears, although it is impossible to be completely sure which is which.

31. Other examples of comedic deafness: Herodas *Mimes* 5.55; Cratinus "Archilochoi" frag. 6, *PCG.*

32. Finley, "The Elderly in Classical Antiquity," 156 and passim, discusses the role of the elderly in comedy.

33. Meyer Reinhold, "The Generation Gap in Antiquity," in *The Conflict of Generations in Ancient Greece and Rome,* ed. S. Bertman (Amsterdam: Grüner, 1976), 44, argues that the conflict of generations is particularly a fifth-century phenomenon.

34. Hanson, *Western Way of War,* 95.

35. Hanson, *Western Way of War,* 147–50, 152–54, reconstructs the chaos and the noise of battle.

36. Jan Bremmer, "The Old Women of Ancient Greece," in *Sexual Asymmetry: Studies in Ancient Society,* ed. Josine Blok and Peter Mason (Amsterdam: J. C. Gieben, 1987), 191–215, has assembled the evidence that exists for old women in general.

37. Rabinowitz, "Female Speech and Female Sexuality," 127–40.

38. Lane, *When the Mind Hears,* 93, writes that "those who were deaf only but could speak—who had established their credentials in the eyes of hearing society and knew their oral language—have always been regarded as persons at law." That those who could speak have "always" been seen as worthwhile is probably true, but

the earliest documentation, as Lane points out, is not until the Code of Justinian, sixth century A.D.

39. The question of nasal speech comes up in Pseudo-Aristotle *Problems* 11.2.899 a. The answer hinges on the relation between deafness and dumbness, followed by a physiological explanation about breath and the tongue, mirroring the Hippocratic corpus (*Fleshes* 8); another connection between deafness and dumbness, followed by an explanation that the nostrils of the deaf are distended because the deaf breathe more violently (11.4.899 a); and a suggestion that deafness is a congestion in the region of the lungs (33.14.962 b). Similarly, Galen (8.267.14–16) describes a condition in which injured throat muscles result in a wounded voice, but specifies that a weak voice, not muteness, results.

40. For present-day statistics, see William Stokoe, "Language, Prelanguage, and Sign Language," *Seminars in Speech and Language* 11 (1990): 93.

Regarding the proportion of the deaf in the ancient world, this is as discussed in chapter 2. Lampropoulou, "The History of Deaf Education in Greece," 240, suggests that deaf babies in Sparta were included among those "with disabilities" and discarded. There is no reason, though, to believe that babies born deaf were subject to exposure, if only because the deafness would not be detected until later, as Danielle Gourevitch, "Un enfant muet de naissance s'exprime par le dessin," *L'Evolution Psychiatrique* 56, no. 4 (1991): 890, points out. It is possible that a child who was perceived as worthless would have received less than his or her share of necessities and thus eventually died, but there is no evidence for or against this.

41. Franklin Silverman, *Communication for the Speechless* (Boston: Allyn and Bacon, 1995), 11. Steven Pinker, *The Language Instinct* (New York: William Morrow and Company, 1994), 37–38, points out that successful language acquisition must take place in childhood and (293) that the likelihood of acquiring spoken language is steadily compromised after the age of six.

42. Alan Boegehold, "Antigone, Nodding, Unbowed," in *The Eye Expanded: Life and the Arts in Greco-Roman Antiquity,* ed. Frances Titchener and Richard Moorton (Berkeley: University of California Press, 1999), 19–23, demonstrates the importance to scholars of ancient Greek of paying attention not only to the written words but also to the implied gestures.

43. Alan Boegehold, *When a Gesture Was Expected: A Selection of Examples from Archaic and Classical Greek Literature* (Princeton: Princeton University Press, 1999), 16.

44. S. Goldin-Meadow and C. Mylander, "The Development of Morphology without a Conventional Language Model," in *From Gesture to Language in Hearing and Deaf Children,* ed. V. Volterra and Carol Erting (New York: Springer, 1990), 165. Lane, *When the Mind Hears,* 5, describes "home sign," a system of abbreviated gestures. Pinker, *Language Instinct,* 36, cites a situation in Nicaragua in the 1970s in which deaf children pooled their gestures and developed what is now a codified system of gestures. Since it is not based on consistent grammar, this system is "basically pidgin."

45. William Stokoe, "Seeing Clearly through Fuzzy Speech," *Sign Language Studies* 82 (spring 1994): 90.

46. Robert E. Johnson and Carol Erting, "Ethnicity and Socialization in a Classroom for Deaf Children," in *The Sociolinguistics of the Deaf Community*, ed. C. Lucas (New York: Academic Press, 1989), 43, 49.

47. M. C. Da Cunha Pereira and C. De Lemos, "Gesture in Hearing Mother–Deaf Child Interaction," in *From Gesture to Language in Hearing and Deaf Children,* ed. V. Volterra and Carol Erting (New York: Springer, 1990), 186.

48. As Chester Starr, *The Economic and Social Growth of Early Greece, 800–500 B.C.* (New York: Oxford University Press, 1977), 152–56, calculates.

49. As Eberhard Ruschenbusch, "Tribut und Bürgerzahl im ersten Athenischen Seebund," *Zeitschrift für Papyrologie und Epigraphik* 53 (1983): 145, estimates.

50. Rosiland Thomas, *Literacy and Orality in Ancient Greece* (Cambridge: Cambridge University Press, 1992), 2–4, discusses the extent of nonliteracy.

51. The tale is recorded in various sources, including the fragments of Sophocles' lost play *Tereus,* frags. 581–95, in A. C. Pearson, ed., *The Fragments of Sophocles* (Cambridge: Cambridge University Press, 1917); Apollodorus 3.14.8; Pausanias 1.41.8–9. Only in Apollodorus's version does Philomela weave written characters, as opposed to images, into her robe.

52. Pseudo-Aristotle (*Problems* 898 b) asks why those who suffer any defect from birth mostly have bad hearing and asks in answer if it is because hearing and voice arise from the same source; he also observes (*Problems* 33.1.961 b) that men become deaf and dumb at the same time. This observation is echoed by Pliny *Natural History* 10.88.192.

53. O'Neill, *Speech and Speech Disorders in Western Thought,* 3–11.

54. Trans. G. Norlin (1928; reprint, Cambridge: Harvard University Press, 1980), 1:147–49.

55. There are many possible interpretations. D. L. Drew, "Euripides' *Alcestis,*" *American Journal of Philology* 52, no. 4 (1931): 295–319, argues that this is the corpse of Alcestis. Whether the figure on stage was meant to be seen as alive, dead, or something in between, Drew points out (313) that even if only three speaking actors were available, her continued silence was not necessary from a technical standpoint. Charles Segal, *Art, Gender, and Communication in* Alcestis, Hippolytus, *and* Hecuba (Durham: Duke University Press, 1993), 49, writes that Alcestis's final silence has associations with death.

56. John Gager, *Curse Tablets and Binding Spells from the Ancient World* (New York: Oxford University Press, 1992), 159–60. Gager (116–50) discusses curses and binding spells in the courtroom.

57. Golden, *Children and Childhood in Classical Athens,* 35–36, discusses the agricultural labor of children—gathering stones from the field, breaking up dirt, tending animals—as a criterion that helps assess their value as an economic unit in the family.

CHAPTER FIVE

1. Herbert C. Covey, *Social Perceptions of People with Disabilities in History* (Springfield, Ill.: Charles C. Thomas, 1998), 192.

2. Similarly, "the two ways in which separation was practiced with the blind are annihilation and veneration." See Berthold Lowenfeld, *The Changing Status of the Blind: From Separation to Integration* (Springfield, Ill.: Charles C. Thomas, 1975), 14. See also Richard Slayton French, *From Homer to Helen Keller: A Social and Educational Study of the Blind* (New York: American Foundation for the Blind,

1932); and C. Edwin Vaughan, *Social and Cultural Perspectives on Blindness: Barriers to Community Integration* (Springfield, Ill.: Charles C. Thomas, 1998), 89.

3. William Paulson, *Enlightenment, Romanticism, and the Blind in France* (Princeton: Princeton University Press, 1987), 3–4.

4. Degrees of blindness are defined by the Social Security Administration.

5. George Sines and Yannis A. Sakellarakis, "Lenses in Antiquity," *American Journal of Archaeology* 91 (1987): 193, write that the concept of magnification was known in Roman times and perhaps used by gem carvers, who were especially subject to eyestrain.

6. Here, Lycurgus is blinded by Zeus as punishment for his having frightened the attendants of Dionysus.

7. Aristotle (*Categories* 10.12 a 35–39; *Topics* 2.2.109 b 22, 5.6.135 b 31–32) contrasts blindness and sight.

8. Seen, for example, in *P. Oxy.* 1.99.9, 10.1276.8, 34.2722 recto 23, 34.2722.65.

9. Richard E. Doyle, 'ATH: *Its Use and Meaning: A Study in the Greek Poetic Tradition from Homer to Euripides* (New York: Fordham University Press, 1984).

10. This is the sole surviving instance of the use of this compound term.

11. In this first surviving appearance of Thamyris, the term is the all-encompassing "maimed" (*pêros*), but as Bernidaki-Aldous, *Blindness in a Culture of Light*, 92, points out, there is no reason to think of the punishment as anything other than blindness, given the long tradition of Thamyris and his punishment from the Muses.

12. Lowenfeld, *Changing Status of the Blind*, 18.

13. Charles Kolk, *Assessment and Planning with the Visually Impaired* (Baltimore: University Park Press, 1981), 6.

14. Bernidaki-Aldous, *Blindness in a Culture of Light*, 61, 80, summarizes the various traditions of Phineus's blinding and being blinded.

15. *Oedipus the King*, trans. Albert Cook, in *Ten Greek Plays in Contemporary Translation*, ed. L. R. Lind (Boston: Houghton Mifflin, 1957), 147.

16. Lowenfeld, *Changing Status of the Blind*, 21; Vaughan, *Social and Cultural Perspectives on Blindness*, 89.

17. The story is repeated in Plutarch *Moralia* 305 c, with the name Polyzelus. Albert Esser, *Das Antlitz der Blindheit in der Antike* (Leiden: E. J. Brill, 1961), 26–27, reasonably interprets this as a case of hysterical blindness.

18. Anticrates was cured.

19. Although the term night blindness (*nuktalôpos*) appears in the Hippocratic corpus (e.g., *On Vision* 9.7), the editor of the Hippocratic corpus, É. Littré, cautions (9.149–50) that there is some confusion in the Hippocratic corpus about what the term meant, medically. Galen (9.124) is the first to define night blindness precisely.

20. The two additional cases of blindness on this stele (233) do not record the cause of blindness.

21. As suggested by Thomas Winter, "Lippus, Lippire, Lippitudo" (paper presented at the annual meeting of the American Philological Association, San Diego, Calif., 29 December 1995).

22. Alfred Sommer, *Nutritional Blindness: Xerophthalmia and Keratomalacia* (New York: Oxford University Press, 1982), 187, writes that sources of vitamin A

have been used as a treatment for night blindness for millennia. Jean Pennington, *Food Values of Portions Commonly Used,* 15th ed. (New York: HarperCollins, 1989), 144, shows that a slice of broiled lamb liver has 33,530 IU of vitamin A. Sommer also reports (191–92) 95 percent of patients improved or healed after treatment consisting of 100,000 IU of vitamin A on the first day of treatment, followed by 200,000 IU of vitamin A the following day.

23. Richard Young, *Age-Related Cataract* (New York: Oxford University Press, 1991), x. Of the twenty-eight million blind people in the world, seventeen million are blind from cataract.

24. Heinrich von Staden, *Herophilus: The Art of Medicine in Early Alexandria* (Cambridge: Cambridge University Press, 1989), 573–74.

25. The writer calls the disease "ophthalmia," which in both modern terms and ancient terms is an inflammation of the eye. It is used in the Hippocratic corpus to refer to many varieties of eye inflammation, not just glaucoma.

26. Ralph Jackson, "Roman Doctors and Their Instruments: Recent Research into Ancient Practice," *Journal of Roman Archaeology* 3 (1990): 12.

27. George Boon, "Potters, Occultists, and Eye-Troubles," *Britannica* 14 (1983): 10.

28. Grmek, *Diseases in the Ancient Greek World,* 128, reads an ancestor of *Staphylococcus aureus* in cases of typical sepsis described in the Hippocratic *Epidemics.*

Grmek (86) does not rule out at least some presence of smallpox in ancient Greece. Morens and Littman, "Epidemiology of the Plague of Athens," 300, cannot rule it out as a possible cause of the plague in 429 B.C. Adam Patrick, "Disease in Antiquity: Greece and Rome," in *Diseases in Antiquity: A Survey of the Diseases, Injuries and Surgery of Early Populations,* ed. Don Brothwell and A. T. Sandison (Springfield, Ill.: Charles C. Thomas, 1967), 239–40, is also unable to rule out the existence of smallpox.

Grmek (148) writes that the vaginal infections described in the Hippocratic writings were caused by *Candida albicans* or by its ancestors.

29. For discussions of trachoma in ancient Greece, see Grmek, *Diseases in the Ancient Greek World,* 26–27; Ronald Hare, "The Antiquity of Diseases Caused by Bacteria and Viruses: A Review of the Problem from a Bacteriologist's Perspective," in *Diseases in Antiquity: A Survey of the Diseases, Injuries and Surgery of Early Populations,* ed. Don Brothwell and A. T. Sandison (Springfield, Ill.: Charles C. Thomas, 1967), 128. Helena Biantovsakya Fedukowicz and Susan Stenson, *External Infections of the Eye: Bacterial, Viral, Mycotic with Noninfectious and Immunologic Diseases,* 3d ed. (Norwalk: Appleton-Century-Crofts, 1985), 83, point out that trachoma still affects about four hundred million people throughout the world and is still a major cause of blindness.

30. Van Straten, "Gifts for the Gods," 105–51, catalogs votive offerings representing body parts in the Greek world.

31. Sara Aleshire, *The Athenian Asklepieion: The People, Their Dedications, and the Inventories* (Amsterdam: J. C. Gieben, 1989), 42.

32. Morens and Littman, "Epidemiology of the Plague of Athens," 271, report that for the Athenian plague, twenty-nine different disease theories have been advanced by hundreds of scholars. They conclude that the possible diseases are

limited to reservoir diseases, the most likely of which would be typhus, arboviral (a virus borne by invertebrate organisms that results in encephalitis), or plague; or respiratory, such as smallpox or, less likely, measles or streptococcal disease (300).

33. Kottek, *Medicine and Hygiene in the Works of Flavius Josephus*, 150–60.

34. Herman de Ley, "Beware of Blue Eyes! A Note on the Hippocratic Pangenesis," *L'Antiquité classique* 50 (1981): 196–97.

35. E. D. Phillips, *Aspects of Greek Medicine* (Philadelphia: Charles Press, 1987), 48, points out that the eye is the only organ described structurally in the Hippocratic corpus. James Longrigg, *Greek Rational Medicine: Philosophy and Medicine from Alcmaeon to the Alexandrians* (New York: Routledge, 1993), 58–60, traces the Greek scientific understanding of the eye to the empirical investigations of Alcmaeon, through Empedocles' discussion of the eye as composed of balanced humors (71–72), through the anatomical research of the Alexandrian Herophilus (193–95).

36. Bernidaki-Aldous, *Blindness in a Culture of Light*, 19–26, discusses the literary motif of sight.

37. As discussed by R. G. A. Buxton, "Blindness and Limits: Sophokles and the Logic of Myth," *Journal of Hellenic Studies* 100 (1980): 23–37. Bernidaki-Aldous, *Blindness in a Culture of Light*, 11–26, discusses blindness as metaphor for death and (49–55) blindness as metaphor for ignorance.

38. George H. Bohigian, "The History of the Evil Eye and Its Influence on Ophthalmology, Medicine, and Social Customs," *Documenta Opthalmologica* 94 (1997): 91.

39. As David Wiles, *Greek Theatre Performance: An Introduction* (Cambridge: Cambridge University Press, 2000), 109, suggests. In the absence of industrial noise, Wiles's suggestion makes sense.

40. *Scent of a Woman,* dir. Martin Brest, 1992, 157 mins.

41. Michael J. Tobin, "Blindness in Later Life: Myths, Attitudes and Reality," *British Journal of Visual Impairment* 13, no. 2 (1995): 69–70.

42. Kathi Wolfe, "Don't Bug Me!" *Mainstream* 20 (April 1996): 25.

43. Garland, *Eye of the Beholder,* 34, discusses the connection between blind people's ordinary reliance on hearing and the special powers perceived in blind people.

44. Tobin, "Blindness in Later Life," 71.

45. This is repeated, but by Teiresias to *his* daughter in Euripides *Phoenician Women* 834. Also see Aristophanes *Wealth* 1–15; and Plutarch *Moralia* 6 a. Ephorus (*FGrH* 70 F 1) tells us that Homer acquired his name along with his blindness, because blind people use guides. Grmek, *Diseases in the Ancient Greek World,* 25, points out that the etymology is false.

46. Johann Peter Krafft (1780–1856), *Oedipus and Antigone at Colonus,* pen and brown ink, brush and brown wash over graphite on off-white wove paper, 46.5 × 34.6 cm., inv. no. 89.65. The Richard Lewis Hillstrom Fund. Reproduced with permission from the Minneapolis Institute of Arts.

47. Lionel Casson, *Travel in the Ancient World* (London: George Allen and Unwin, 1974), 94.

48. John Hull, *Touching the Rock: An Experience of Blindness* (New York: Pantheon, 1990), 102–3.

49. As Anne Pippin Burnett, "Hekabe the Dog," *Arethusa* 27 (spring 1994): 153, points out.

50. Margaret Louck, "Cultivating the Body: Anthropology and Epistemologies of Bodily Practice and Knowledge," *Annual Review of Anthropology* 22 (1993): 138.

51. We know pitifully little about blind women in ancient Greece. I have yet to come across a reference to a blind woman. Women would have been less subject to eye injury by trauma, but otherwise they would have been as vulnerable to any other cause of blindness.

52. Bernidaki-Aldous, *Blindness in a Culture of Light*, 39, believes that Polymestor's blinding, though justly invoked, roused pity in the audience.

53. Vaughan, *Social and Cultural Perspectives on Blindness*, 89.

54. See Bernidaki-Aldous, *Blindness in a Culture of Light*, 6; Garland, *Eye of the Beholder*, 33.

Plutarch *Pelopidas* 3.4 describes Pelopidas's scorn for money as he points to a lame and blind man as an example of the sort of creature who needs money or, in other words, is not self-sufficient. Diogenes Laertius *Diogenes* 56 implies that people give money to beggars because they think they themselves may become lame or blind some day. Another possible example is seen in Philostratus *Life of Apollonius* 4.10, where a beggar is perhaps pretending to be blind—he is "craftily winking his eyes."

55. French, *From Homer to Helen Keller*, 34.

56. The life of Didymus the Blind is summarized by Johannes Leipoldt, *Didymus der Blinde von Alexandria* (Leipzig: J. C. Hinrich, 1905).

57. Ada Adler, ed., *Suidae Lexicon*, 4 vols. (Leipzig, 1928–35; reprint, Stuttgart: Teubner, 1967–71), s.v. Eratosthenês. According to this late (tenth-century) source, Eratosthenes starved himself to death because of his failing sight.

58. As we see, for example, in the Homeric Hymn *To Apollo* (170–72), where the unknown author has Homer ask to be remembered as the blind man from Chios. Grmek, *Diseases in the Ancient Greek World*, 25–27, concludes that a case could be made either way for Homer's blindness or sight.

59. Kathi Wolfe, "The Write Stuff," *Mainstream* 21 (October 1996): 32–34.

60. Diana Trilling, "Reading by Ear," *Civilization* 1 (November/December 1994): 54.

61. William Harris, *Ancient Literacy* (Cambridge: Harvard University Press, 1989), 111, discusses literate slaves.

62. Plutarch *Moralia* 440 a–b repeats the story.

63. As discussed by Hanson, *Western Way of War*, 152–53.

64. Monika Helbing, "Der Altägyptische Augenkranke, sein Arzt und seine Götter," *Zürcher Medizingeschichtliche Abhandlungen* 141 (1980): 69, notes that blind people had a special place as gatekeepers in Egyptian folk tales.

65. Baldwin, "Medical Grounds for Exemption from Military Service," 43.

66. Marcus M. Tod, "An Ephebic Inscription from Memphis," *Journal of Egyptian Archaeology* 37 (1951): 86–99.

67. David Schaps, "The Women of Greece in Wartime," *Classical Philology* 77 (1982): 194.

1. Finley, "The Elderly in Classical Antiquity," 156–71.

2. Christopher Carey, "Structure and Strategy in Lysias XXIV," *Greece and Rome* 37 (1990): 50, n. 3, argues that there is no basis for precise dating of this speech. Kenneth Dover, *Lysias and the Corpus Lysiacum* (Berkeley: University of California Press, 1968), 189, concludes that, linguistically, there is no reason to think that this speech, Lysias 24, is not genuine. Carey, "Structure and Strategy in Lysias XXIV," 50, also assumes that the speech was intended to be read before the Boule.

3. Plutarch *Solon* 31 probably refers to the origins of this dole when reporting the Athenian law—that anyone maimed in war should be maintained by the state—as one that the sixth-century tyrant Peisistratus devised. Plutarch tells us that the fourth-century B.C. writer Heracleides of Pontus offers a conflicting report in which Peisistratus's law was not original but based on Solon's support of one such man maimed in war, Thersippus. Fritz Wehrli, *Herakleides Pontikos,* Texte und Kommentar 7, *Der Schule des Aristoteles* (Basel: Benno Schwabe, 1953), 110, discusses this statement of Heracleides of Pontus (frag. 149) as an example of trying to attribute all good things to Solon the Sage, the Solon of Herodotus. That Plutarch's account of the origins of the dole (*Solon* 31), the dole in Lysias 24, and the law described by the author of the *Athenian Constitution* (49.4) all describe the same thing is basically agreed on by Hands, *Charities and Social Aid in Greece and Rome,* 137–38; Garland, *Eye of the Beholder,* 36; and Rhodes, *Commentary on the Aristotelian* Athenaion Politeia, 570.

4. Matthew Dillon, "Payments to the Disabled at Athens: Social Justice or Fear of Aristocratic Patronage?" *Ancient Society* 26 (1995): 57.

5. Carey, "Structure and Strategy in Lysias XXIV," summarizes the speech and analyzes the structure, concluding (48–49) that because the defendant does not have a strong case, Lysias has him rely on "verbal guerilla tactics" instead.

6. Dasen, *Dwarfs in Ancient Egypt and Greece,* 212, suggests that there was an "unwritten religious taboo" against people with physical disabilities holding office and finds confirmation in the absence of reference to handicapped officials of sacred functions except for Medon, the legendary ruler of Athens, who, Pausanias 7.2.1 tells us, was given Athens by the Delphic oracle after his brother tried to deny him the rule because Medon was lame in the foot. Perhaps, though, there was no reason to point out that an office holder had a physical handicap unless, as in this legendary case, it was relevant.

7. As Garland, *Eye of the Beholder,* 37, notes.

8. As Stiker, *Corps infirmes et sociétés,* 59, points out.

9. Juan Alejandro Ré, *El Problema de la Mendicidad en Buenos Aires: Sus Causas y Remedios* (Buenos Aires: Talleres Gráficos Argentinos, 1938), 21–22, discusses the impersonator; Rosa Maria Perez Estevez, *El Problema de los Vagos en la España del Siglo XVIII* (Madrid: Confederacion Española de Cajas Ahorros, 1976), 57–58, also contrasts legitimate beggars on one hand and beggars disguised to look needy on the other.

10. Hands, *Charities and Social Aid in Greece and Rome,* 77–78. We see disguises of disability in Greek literature, but the disguises never induce pity and alms, nor are they meant to. Odysseus's disguise (Homer *Odyssey* 17.202–4) gets him

anything but pity; the despicable Aristogeiton's sham, seen in Plutarch *Phocion* 10.1–2, only gets him out of military service.

11. Carey, "Structure and Strategy in Lysias XXIV," 50, points out that "for riding in ancient Greece strong thighs were essential, yet our speaker is supposedly disabled in his legs." Because the defendant could mount and ride a horse, though, does not preclude any number of physical handicaps involving the legs. For all we know, he had clubfeet; was missing one or both feet or lower legs; or was affected by multiple sclerosis, the symptoms of which are sporadic, varying with factors such as heat.

References ॐ

PRIMARY SOURCES

Adler, Ada, ed. *Suidae Lexicon*. 4 vols. Leipzig: 1928–35. Reprint, Stuttgart: Teubner, 1967–71.

Aeschines. Edited by Udalricus Schindel. Stuttgart: Teubner, 1978.

Aeschylus. Translated by Herbert Smith. 2 vols. Loeb Classical Library. Cambridge: Harvard University Press, 1973–83.

Angel, J. Lawrence. "Ancient Greek Skeletal Change." *American Journal of Physical Anthropology* 4 (1946): 69–97.

———. "Ancient Skeletons from Asine." In *General Stratigraphical Analysis and Architectural Remains: Asine II: Results of the Excavations East of the Acropolis, 1970–1974*, edited by S. Dietz, fasc. 1, 105–38. Stockholm: Paul Aströms, 1982.

———. "Geometric Athenians." In *Late Geometric Graves and a Well in the Agora*, edited by S. Young, 236–46. The American Excavations in the Athenian Agora. *Hesperia*, supplement 2. Athens: The American School of Classical Studies at Athens, 1939.

———. *The People of Lerna: Analysis of a Prehistoric Aegean Population*. Princeton: American School of Classical Studies at Athens; Washington, D.C.: Smithsonian Institution Press, 1971.

———. "Skeletal Material from Attica." *Hesperia* 14 (1945): 279–363.

Apollodorus. Translated by G. Frazer. 2 vols. Loeb Classical Library. Cambridge: Harvard University Press, 1976–79.

Apollonius Rhodius. *Argonautica*. Translated by R. C. Seaton. Loeb Classical Library. Cambridge: Harvard University Press, 1980.

Aristophanes. Translated by B. B. Rogers. 3 vols. 1924. Loeb Classical Library. Cambridge: Harvard University Press, 1963–82.

Aristotle. Translated by G. Cyril Armstrong, Harold P. Cooke, Francis M. Cornford, E. S. Forster, John Henry Freese, D. J. Furley, W. Hamilton Fyfe, W. K. C. Guthrie, W. S. Hett, H. D. P. Lee, A. L. Peck, H. Rackham, Hugh Trednnick, and Philip H. Wickstead. 23 vols. Loeb Classical Library. 1926–60. Reprint, Cambridge: Harvard University Press, 1966–87.

Athenaeus. Translated by C. Gulick. 7 vols. Loeb Classical Library. Cambridge: Harvard University Press, 1927–41.

Betz, Hans D. *The Greek Magical Papyri in Translation*. Chicago: University of Chicago Press, 1986.

Bidez, J. *Vie de Porphye le philosophe néo-platonicien*. Hildesheim: George Olds, 1964.

Bräuer, G., and R. Fricke. "Zur Phänomenologie osteoporotischer Veränderungen bei Bestehen systemischen hämatologischer Affektionen." *Homo* 31 (1980): 198–211.

Celsus. Translated by W. G. Spencer. 3 vols. Loeb Classical Library. Cambridge: Harvard University Press, 1971.

Charles, Robert P. "Étude anthropologique des nécropoles d'Argos." *Bulletin des correspondance hellénique* 82 (1958): 268–313.

Cicero. Translated by D. R. Shackleton Baley, Henry Caplan, William Armstead Falconer, John Henry Freese, R. Gardner, L. H. G. Greenwood, G. L. Henderson, Mary Henderson, H. M. Hubbell, Walter C. A. Ker, Clinton Walker Keyes, J. E. King, E. Macdonald, Walter Miller, H. Rackham, E. W. Sutton, N. H. Watts, W. Glynn Williams, and E. O. Winsteadt. 28 vols. Loeb Classical Library. 1912–72. Reprint, Cambridge: Harvard University Press, 1969–2002.

Coles, R. A., M. W. Haslam, and P. J. Parsons. *The Oxyrhynchus Papyri*, vol. 60. London: Egypt Exploration Society, 1994.

Cunningham, I. C. *Herodas Miamiambi*. Oxford: Clarendon Press, 1971.

Quintus Curtius Rufus. *History of Alexander*. Translated by J. C. Rolfe. 2 vols. Loeb Classical Library. Cambridge: Harvard University Press, 1985.

Demosthenes. Translated by Norman J. DeWitt, Norman T. DeWitt, A. T. Murray, C. A. Vince, and J. H. Vince. 7 vols. Loeb Classical Library. 1926–49. Reprint, Cambridge: Harvard University Press, 1962–89.

Diodorus Siculus. Translated by C. Oldfather. 12 vols. Loeb Classical Library. Cambridge: Harvard University Press, 1933–67.

Diogenes Laertius. Translated by R. D. Hicks. 2 vols. Loeb Classical Library. Cambridge: Harvard University Press, 1979.

Dittenberger, W., ed. *Sylloge Inscriptionum Graecarum*, fol 3. Hildesheim: Georg Olms, 1960.

Edelstein, Emma, and Ludwig Edelstein. *Asclepius: A Collection and Interpretation of the Testimonies*. 2 vols. Baltimore: Johns Hopkins University Press, 1945.

Euripides. Translated by A. Way. 4 vols. Loeb Classical Library. Cambridge: Harvard University Press, 1988.

———. *Alcestis*. Edited by A. M. Dale. Oxford: Clarendon Press, 1987.

———. *Medea and Other Plays*. Translated by Philip Vellacott. New York: Penguin, 1963.

———. *Orestes*. Edited by G. Murray. 2d ed. 3 vols. Oxford: Clarendon Press, 1978.

Gager, John. *Curse Tablets and Binding Spells from the Ancient World*. New York: Oxford University Press, 1992.

Galen. *Medicorum Graecorum*. Edited by D. Carolus Gottlob Kühn. 20 vols. Leipzig: Knobloch, 1821.

Gejvall, N-G., and F. Henschen. "Two Late Roman Skeletons with Malformation and Close Family Relationship from Ancient Corinth." *Opuscula Athenesia* 8 (1968): 179–93.

Grenfell, B. P., and Arthur Hunt, eds. *The Oxyrhynchus Papyri*, vol. 1. London: Egypt Exploration Society, 1898.

———. *The Oxyrhynchus Papyri*, vol. 10. London: Egypt Exploration Society, 1914.

———. *The Oxyrhynchus Papyri*, vol. 12. London: Egypt Exploration Society, 1916.

Grenfell, B. P., Arthur Hunt, and H. I. Bell, eds. *The Oxyrhynchus Papyri*, vol. 16. London: Egypt Exploration Society, 1924.

Henneberg, Maciej, and Renata Henneberg. "Biological Characteristics of the Population Based on an Analysis of Skeletal Remains." In *The Chora of Metaponto: The Necropoleis*, edited by J. Coleman Carter, 2:503–59. Austin: Institute of Classical Archaeology, 1998.

Hermogenes. Edited by H. Rabe. Leipzig, 1913. Reprint, Stuttgart: Teubner, 1969.

Herodas. *Mimes.* In *Theophrastus, Characters; Herodas, Mimes; Cercidas and the Choliambic Poets,* edited and translated by I. C. Cunningham, 74–176. Loeb Classical Library. Cambridge: Harvard University Press, 1993.

Herodotus. Translated by A. D. Godley. 4 vols. Loeb Classical Library. Cambridge: Harvard University Press, 1982–90.

Hesiod. Edited by Friedrich Solmson. 3d ed. Oxford: Clarendon Press, 1990.

———. *The Homeric Hymns and Homerica.* Translated by H. Evelyn-White. Loeb Classical Library. Cambridge: Harvard University Press, 1977.

Homer. *Iliad.* Translated by A. T. Murray. 2 vols. Loeb Classical Library. Cambridge: Harvard University Press, 1924–25.

———. *Iliad.* Translated by Richmond Lattimore. Chicago: University of Chicago Press, 1976.

———. *Odyssey.* Translated by A. T. Murray. Cambridge: 1919. 2 vols. Loeb Classical Library. Reprint, Cambridge: Harvard University Press, 1984–91.

Hunt, Arthur, ed. *Selected Papyri.* Loeb Classical Library. Cambridge: Harvard University Press, 1950.

Hunt, Arthur, and G. Smyly, eds. *The Tebtunis Papyri*, vol. 3, part 1. London: Egypt Exploration Society, 1933.

Husselman, Elinor Mullett, Arthur E. R. Boak, and William F. Edgerton, eds. *Papyri from Tebtunis,* part 2. Michigan Papyri, no. 5. Ann Arbor: University of Michigan Press, 1944.

Ingrams, L., P. Kingston, P. Parson, and J. Rea, eds. *The Oxyrhynchus Papyri*, vol. 34. London: Egypt Exploration Society, 1968.

Isocrates. Translated by G. Norlin and La Rue van Hook. Cambridge, 1928–45. Reprint, 3 vols. Loeb Classical Library. Cambridge: Harvard University Press, 1980–86.

Jacoby, Felix. *Die Fragmente der Griechischen Historiker.* 3 vols. Leiden: E. J. Brill, 1923–94.

Kassel, R., and C. Austin, eds. *Poetae Comici Graeci,* 7 vols. Berlin: Walter de Gruyter, 1983–86.

Kock, T., ed. *Comicorum Atticorum Fragmenta*, vol. 2. Leipzig: Teubner, 1884.

The Letters of Alciphron, Aelian, and Philostratus. Translated by A. R. Benner and

F. H. Fobes. Loeb Classical Library. Cambridge: Harvard University Press, 1949.

Lexicon Iconographicum Mythologiae Classica, vol. 4, *Eros-Herakles,* parts 1 and 2. Zurich: Artemis, 1988.

Lind, L. R., ed. *Ten Greek Plays in Contemporary Translation.* Boston: Houghton Mifflin, 1957.

Littré, É., ed. *Oeuvres Complètes D'Hippocrate.* 10 vols. Paris: Ballière, 1839–61.

Lobel, E., E. P. Wegener, C. H. Roberts, and H. I. Bell, eds. *The Oxyrhynchus Papyri,* vol. 19. London: Egypt Exploration Society, 1948.

López Jimeno, Amor, and Jesús Nieto Ibáñez. "Nueva Lectura de una *Defixio* de Selinunte (*SEG* XXVII 1115)." *Emerita* 57 (1989): 325–27.

Lucian. Translated by A. M. Harmon. 8 vols. Loeb Classical Library. Cambridge: Harvard University Press, 1913–67.

Lysias. Edited by C. Hude. Oxford: Clarendon Press, n.d.

Page, D. L. *Poetae Melici Graeci.* Oxford: Clarendon Press, 1962.

Paton, William, ed. and trans. *The Greek Anthology.* 5 vols. Loeb Classical Library. Cambridge: Harvard University Press, 1916–18.

Pausanias. Translated by W. H. S. Jones. 4 vols. Loeb Classical Library. Cambridge: Harvard University Press, 1918–55.

Pearson, A. C., ed. *The Fragments of Sophocles.* Cambridge: Cambridge University Press, 1917.

Petzl, Georg, ed. *Die Inschriften von Smyrna.* Inschriften Griechischer Stadte Aus Kleinasien, no. 23. 2 vols. Bonn: Rudolf Habelt, 1982.

Philostratus Major. *Imagines.* Edited by O. Benndorf and K. Schenkl. Leipzig: Teubner, 1893.

Flavius Philostratus. *The Life of Apollonius of Tyana.* Translated by F. Conybeare. 2 vols. Loeb Classical Library. Cambridge: Harvard University Press, 1969.

Pindar. Translated by John Sandys. Loeb Classical Library. Cambridge: Harvard University Press, 1978.

Plato. Translated by R. G. Bury. 12 vols. Loeb Classical Library. Cambridge: Harvard University Press, 1925–98.

Pleket, H. W., and R. S. Stroud, eds. *Supplementum Epigraphicum Graecum.* 36 vols. Alphen aan den Rijn: Sijtholf and Woordhoff, 1923–.

Pliny. *Natural History.* Translated by H. Rackman. 10 vols. Loeb Classical Library. Cambridge: Harvard University Press, 1942–83.

Plutarch. *Lives.* Translated by B. Perrin. 1914–26. 11 vols. Loeb Classical Library. Reprint, Cambridge: Harvard University Press, 1967–86.

———. *Moralia.* Translated by F. C. Babbit, H. Cherniss, P. A. Clement, P. H. DeLacy, B. Einarson, H. N. Fowler, W. C. Helmbold, H. B. Hoffleit, E. L. Minar, Jr., Lionel Pearson, and F. H. Sandbach. 15 vols. Loeb Classical Library. 1931–76. Reprint, Cambridge: Harvard University Press, 1969–89.

Polybius. Translated by W. R. Paton. 6 vols. Loeb Classical Library. Cambridge: Harvard University Press, 1922–1927.

Positano, Lydia, D. Holwerda, and W. J. W. Koster, eds. *Commentarium In Nubes.* Jo. Tzetzae Commentarii in Aristophanem, no. 4:2. Groningem: Bouma, 1960.

Quintilian. Translated by H. E. Butler. 4 vols. Loeb Classical Library. Cambridge: Harvard University Press, 1920–80.

Rea, J. R., ed. *The Oxyrhynchus Papyri,* vol. 51. London: Egypt Exploration Society, 1984.

——. *The Oxyrhynchus Papyri,* vol. 55. London: Egypt Exploration Society, 1988.

Richter, Gisela M. A. *Catalogue of Greek and Roman Antiquities in the Dumbarton Oaks Collection.* Dumbarton Oaks Catalogues. Cambridge: Harvard University Press, 1956.

Sophocles. Translated by F. Storr. 2 vols. Loeb Classical Library. Cambridge: Harvard University Press, 1951–94.

Soranus. *Gynecology.* Translated by Oswei Temkin. Baltimore: Johns Hopkins University Press, 1991.

Strabo. *Geography.* Translated by H. Jones. 9 vols. Loeb Classical Library. Cambridge: Harvard University Press, 1917–33.

Theophrastus. *Characters.* Translated by J. M. Edmonds. Loeb Classical Library. Cambridge: Harvard University Press, 1961.

——. *On the Causes of Plants.* Translated by B. Einarson and George K. K. Link. 3 vols. Loeb Classical Library. Cambridge: Harvard University Press, 1976–90.

Thucydides. Translated by C. Smith. 4 vols. Loeb Classical Library. Cambridge: 1919–23. Reprint, Cambridge: Harvard University Press, 1986–91.

Tod, Marcus M. "An Ephebic Inscription from Memphis." *Journal of Egyptian Archaeology* 37 (1951): 86–99.

——, ed. *Greek Historical Inscriptions From the Sixth Century BC to the Death of Alexander the Great in 323 BC.* Two Volumes in One. 1946, 1948. Reprint, Chicago: Ares, 1985.

Xenophon. Translated by C. Brownson, E. C. Marchant, W. Miller, and O. J. Todd. 7 vols. Loeb Classical Library. 1914–23. Reprint, Cambridge: Harvard University Press, 1979–86.

Wade, William. "The Dark Age: Burials." In *Excavations at Nichoria in Southwest Greece,* vol. 3, edited by W. A. McDonald, W. D. E. Coulson, and J. Rosser, 260–72. Minneapolis: University of Minnesota Press, 1983.

Wehrli, Fritz. *Heraklides Pontikos.* Texte und Kommentar 7, *Der Schule des Aristoteles.* Basel: Benno Schwabe, 1953.

West, M. L., ed. *Iambi et Elegi Graeci.* 2d ed. 2 vols. Oxford: Clarendon Press, 1989.

Youtie, Herbert, and Orasmus Pearl, eds. *Papyri and Ostraca from Karanis.* Michigan Papyri, no. 6. Humanistic Series, no. 47. Ann Arbor: University of Michigan Press, 1944.

——. *Tax Rolls from Karanis.* Michigan Papyri, no. 4.2. Humanistic Series, no. 42. Ann Arbor: University of Michigan Press, 1936.

SECONDARY MATERIAL

Abrams, Judith. *Judaism and Disability: Portrayals in Ancient Texts from the Tanach through the Bavli.* Washington, D.C.: Gallaudet University Press, 1998.

Aitchison, Diana. "Medical Miracles Raise Questions about the Value of Life, the Cost of Care." *St. Louis Post Dispatch,* 13 January 2001, A1+.

Aleshire, Sara. *The Athenian Asklepion: The People, Their Dedications, and the Inventories.* Amsterdam: Gieben, 1989.

Amundsen, Darrel W. "Medicine and the Birth of Defective Children: Approaches of the Ancient World." In *Euthanasia and the Newborn: Conflicts Regarding Saving Lives,* edited by R. McMillan, H. Tristram Engelhardt, Jr., and Stuart F. Spicker, 3–22. Philosophy and Medicine, no. 24. Dordrecht: D. Reidl Publishing Company, 1987.

"Ancient Sparta." Available at <http://encarta.msn.com/find/Concise.> Accessed January 2001.

Armstrong, Linda. "Assessing the Older Communication-Impaired Person." In *Assessment in Speech and Language Therapy,* edited by J. Beech and L. Harding, 163–74. London: Routledge, 1993.

Aterman, Kurt. "From Horus the Child to Hephaestus Who Limps: A Romp through History." *American Journal of Medical Genetics* 83, no. 1 (1999): 53–63.

Avery, Mary Ellen, and Georgia Litwack. *Born Early.* Boston: Little, Brown, and Company, 1983.

Baldwin, Barry. "Medical Grounds for Exemptions from Military Service at Athens." *Classical Philology* 62 (1967): 42–43.

Bartsocas, C. S. "La Génétique dans l'antiquité grecque." *Journal de génétique humaine* 36, no. 4 (1988): 279–93.

Baynton, Douglas. *Forbidden Signs: American Culture and the Campaign against Sign Language.* Chicago: University of Chicago Press, 1996.

Bazopoulou-Kyrkanidou, Euterpe. "What Makes Hephaestus Lame?" *American Journal of Medical Genetics* 72, no. 2 (1997): 144–55.

Benninger, Michael, and Glendon Gardner. "Medical and Surgical Management in Otolaryngology." In *Medical Speech-Language Pathology: A Practitioner's Guide,* edited by Alex Johnson and Barbara Jacobson, 500–502. New York: Theme, 1998.

Berger, Kathleen Stassen. *The Developing Person through Childhood.* 2d ed. New York: Worth Publishing, 2000.

Bernidaki-Aldous, Eleftheria. *Blindness in a Culture of Light: Especially in the Case of Oedipus at Colonus of Sophocles.* New York: Peter Lang, 1990.

Bliquez, Lawrence. "Classical Prosthetics." *Archaeology* 36, no. 5 (Sept. /Oct. 1983): 25–29.

———. "Greek and Roman Medicine." *Archaeology* 34, no. 2 (1981): 10–17.

Bloodstein, Oliver. *A Handbook on Stuttering.* 5th ed. San Diego: Singular Publishing Group, 1995.

Boegehold, Alan. "Antigone, Nodding, Unbowed." In *The Eye Expanded: Life and the Arts in Greco-Roman Antiquity,* edited by Frances Titchener and Richard Moorton, 19–23. Berkeley: University of California Press, 1999.

———. *When a Gesture Was Expected: A Selection of Examples from Archaic and Classical Greek Literature.* Princeton: Princeton University Press, 1999.

Bogdan, Robert. *Freak Show: Presenting Human Oddities for Amusement and Profit.* Chicago: University of Chicago Press, 1988.

Bohigian, George H. "The History of the Evil Eye and Its Influence on Ophthalmology, Medicine, and Social Customs." *Documenta Ophthalmologica* 94 (1997): 91–100.

Bolkenstien, H. "The Exposure of Children at Athens and the *egxutristriai:* Preliminary Note." *Classical Philology* 27 (1922): 222–39.

Boon, George. "Potters, Occultists and Eye-Troubles." *Britannica* 14 (1983): 1–12.

Boswell, John. *The Kindness of Strangers: The Abandonment of Children in Western Europe from Late Antiquity to the Renaissance.* New York: Pantheon, 1988.

Bremmer, Jan. "The Old Women of Ancient Greece." In *Sexual Asymmetry: Studies in Ancient Society,* edited by Josine Blok and Peter Mason, 191–215. Amsterdam: Gieben, 1987.

———. "Scapegoat Rituals in Ancient Greece." In *Oxford Readings in Greek Religion,* edited by R. G. A. Buxton, 271–93. Oxford: Oxford University Press, 2000.

Bridler, René. "Das Trauma in der Kunst der griechischen Antike." Ph.D. diss., Universität Zürich, 1990.

Brock, Roger. "The Labour of Women in Classical Athens." *Classical Quarterly* 44, no. 2 (1994): 336–46.

Brothwell, Don, and Patricia Brothwell. *Food in Antiquity: A Survey of the Diet of Early Peoples.* Ancient People and Places, no. 66. London: Thames and Hudson, 1969.

Burford, Alison. *Craftsmen in Greek and Roman Society.* Aspects of Greek and Roman Life. Ithaca: Cornell University Press, 1972.

Burnett, Anne Pippin. "Hekabe the Dog." *Arethusa* 27 (spring 1994): 151–64.

Buxton, R. G. A. "Blindness and Limits: Sophokles and the Logic of Myth." *Journal of Hellenic Studies* 100 (1980): 22–37.

Byl, Simon. "Rheumatism and Gout in the *Corpus Hippocraticum.*" *L'Antiquite classique* 57 (1988): 89–102.

Cameron, A. "The Exposure of Children and Greek Ethics." *Classical Review* 46 (1932): 105–14.

Carey, Christopher. Introduction to and commentary on *Selected Speeches,* by Lysias. Cambridge: Cambridge University Press, 1989.

———. "Structure and Strategy in Lysias XXIV." *Greece and Rome* 37 (April 1990): 44–51.

Carlson, Earl R. *Born That Way.* New York: John Day, 1941.

Carrick, Paul. *Medical Ethics in Antiquity: Philosophical Perspectives on Abortion and Euthanasia.* Dordrecht: D. Reidl Publishing Company, 1985.

Casson, Lionel. *Travel in the Ancient World.* London: George Allen and Unwin, 1974.

Cohen, M. Michael, and Robert J. Gorlin. "Epidemiology, Etiology, and Genetic Patterns." In *Hereditary Hearing Loss and Its Syndromes,* edited by Robert J. Gorlin, H. Toriello, and M. Michael Cohen, 9–21. Oxford Monographs on Medical Genetics, no. 28. New York: Oxford University Press, 1995.

Corvisier, Jean-Nicolas. *Santé et société en Grèce ancienne.* Paris: Economica, 1985.

Covey, Herbert C. *Social Perceptions of People with Disabilities in History.* Springfield, Ill.: Charles C. Thomas, 1998.

Dasen, Veronique. *Dwarfs in Ancient Egypt and Greece.* Oxford Monographs on Classical Archaeology. Oxford: Clarendon Press, 1993.

Davidson, Paul T., and Enrique Fernandez. "Bone and Joint Tuberculosis." In *Tuberculosis,* edited by D. Schlossberg, 165–78. 3d ed. New York: Springer, 1994.

Davis, Lennard. "Dr. Johnson, Ameila, and the Discourse of Disability." In *"Defects": Engendering the Modern Body,* edited by H. Deutsch and F. Nussbaum, 54–74. Ann Arbor: University of Michigan Press, 2000.

———. *Enforcing Normalcy: Disability, Deafness and the Body.* London: Verso, 1995.

Dawson, Warren R. "Herodotus as a Medical Writer." *Bulletin of the Institute of Classical Studies* 33 (1986): 87–96.

Dean-Jones, Lesley. *Women's Bodies in Classical Greek Science.* Oxford: Oxford University Press, 1994.

de Ley, Herman. "Beware of Blue Eyes! A Note on the Hippocratic Pangenesis." *L'Antiquite classique* 50 (1981): 192–97.

Demand, Nancy. *Birth, Death, and Motherhood in Classical Greece.* Baltimore: Johns Hopkins University Press, 1994.

"Demosthenes." Available at <http://encarta.msn.com/index/conciseindex /6b/06ba7000.htm.>. Accessed June 1999.

Dewald, Carolyn. "Women and Culture in Herodotus' *Histories.*" In *Reflections of Women in Antiquity,* edited by H. Foley, 91–125. New York: Gordon and Breach Science Publishers, 1981.

Dickemann, Mildred. "Concepts and Classification in the Study of Human Infanticide: Sectional Introduction and Some Cautionary Notes." In *Infanticide: Comparative and Evolutionary Perspectives,* edited by Glenn Haufater and Sarah Blaffer Hrdy, 427–37. New York: Aldine Publishing Company, 1984.

Dillon, Matthew. "Payments to the Disabled at Athens: Social Justice or Fear of Aristocratic Patronage?" *Ancient Society* 26 (1995): 27–57.

Dionisopolous-Mass, Regina. "The Evil Eye and Bewitchment in a Peasant Village." In *The Evil Eye,* edited by C. Maloney, 42–62. New York: Columbia University Press, 1976.

Dover, Kenneth J. *Lysias and the* Corpus Lysiacum. Sather Classical Lectures, no. 39. Berkeley: University of California Press, 1968.

Doyle, Richard E. 'ATH: *Its Use and Meaning: A Study in the Greek Poetic Tradition from Homer to Euripides.* New York: Fordham University Press, 1984.

Drew, D. L. "Euripides' *Alcestis.*" *American Journal of Philology* 52, no. 4 (1931): 295–319.

Eldridge, Margaret. *A History of the Treatment of Speech Disorders.* Edinburgh: E. and S. Livingstone, 1968.

Engels, Donald. "The Problem of Female Infanticide in the Greco-Roman World." *Classical Philology* 75 (1980): 112–20.

Esser, Albert. *Das Antlitz der Blindheit in der Antike.* Leiden: E. J. Brill, 1961.

Étienne, Robert. "Ancient Medical Conscience and the Life of Children." Translated by Michèle Morris. *Journal of Psychohistory* 4 (1977): 131–61.

Evans, J. A. S. *Herodotus: Explorer of the Past.* Princeton: Princeton University Press, 1991.

Eyben, Emeil. "Family Planning in Graeco-Roman Antiquity." *Ancient Society* 11–12 (1980–81): 5–82.

Fay, Temple, Jack L. Benson, L. Arnold Post, and Reuben Goldberg. "The Head:

A Neurosurgeon's Analysis of a Great Stone Portrait." *Expedition* 1, no. 4 (1958–59): 12–18.

Fedukowicz, Helena Biantovsakya, and Susan Stenson. *External Infections of the Eye: Bacterial, Viral, Mycotic with Noninfectious and Immunologic Diseases*. 3d ed. Norwalk: Appleton-Century-Crofts, 1985.

Ferris, Jim. "Poems with Disabilities." *Ragged Edge* 21 (March/April 2000): 26.

Filipczak, Zirka Z. *Hot Dry Men, Cold Wet Women: The Theory of Humors in Western European Art, 1575–1700*. New York: The American Federation of Arts, 1997.

Finley, Moses I. "The Elderly in Classical Antiquity." *Greece and Rome* 28, no. 2 (October 1981): 156–71.

French, Richard Slayton. *From Homer to Helen Keller: A Social and Educational Study of the Blind*. New York: American Foundation for the Blind, 1932.

Garland, Robert. "Countdown to the Beginning of Time-Keeping." *History Today* 49 (April 1999): 36–42.

———. *The Eye of the Beholder: Deformity and Disability in the Graeco-Roman World*. Ithaca: Cornell University Press, 1995.

———. "The Mockery of the Deformed and Disabled in Graeco-Roman Culture." In *Laughter Down the Centuries*, edited by S. Jäkel and A. Timonen, 1:71–84. Turku, Finland: Turun Yliopisto, 1994.

Garnsey, Peter. *Food and Society in Classical Antiquity*. Cambridge: Cambridge University Press, 1999.

Gentili, Bruno. *Poetry and Its Public in Ancient Greece from Homer to the Fifth Century*. Translated by A. Thomas Cole. Baltimore: Johns Hopkins University Press, 1988.

Golden, Mark. "Baby Talk and Child Language in Ancient Greece." In *Lo Spettacolo delle Voci*, edited by Francesco de Martino and Alan H. Sommerstein, 11–34. Bari: Levante, 1995.

———. *Children and Childhood in Classical Athens*. Baltimore: Johns Hopkins University Press, 1990.

———. "Demography and the Exposure of Girls at Athens." *Phoenix* 35 (1981): 316–30.

Goldin-Meadow, S., and C. Mylander. "The Development of Morphology without a Conventional Language Model." In *From Gesture to Language in Hearing and Deaf Children*, edited by V. Volterra and Carol Erting, 165–77. New York: Springer, 1990.

Gomme, A. W. *The Population of Athens in the Fifth and Fourth Centuries B.C.* 1933. Reprint, Chicago: Argonaut, 1967.

Gonick, Larry. *The Cartoon History of Universe, Volumes 1–7: From the Big Bang to Alexander the Great*. New York: Doubleday, 1990.

Goodman, Richard M., and Robert J. Gorlin. *The Malformed Infant and Child: An Illustrated Guide*. New York: Oxford University Press, 1983.

Gourevitch, Danielle. "L'Aphonie hippocratique." In *Formes de pensée dans la Collection hippocratique: Actes du IVᵉ Colloque International Hippocratique (Lausanne, 21–26 Septembre 1981)*, edited by F. Lasserre and P. Mudry, 297–305. Geneva: Librairie Droz, 1983.

———. "Un enfant muet de naissance s'exprime par le dessin: À propos d'un cas rapporté par Pline l'Ancien." *L'Evolution Psychiatrique* 56, no. 4 (1991): 889–93.

————. *Le mal d'être femme: La femme et la medecine dans la Rome antique*. Paris: Societe d'edition "Les Belles Lettres," 1984.

Gravel, Pierre Bettez. *The Malevolent Eye: An Essay on the Evil Eye, Fertility and the Concept of Mana*. Anthropology and Sociology, no. 64. New York: Peter Lang, 1995.

Grmek, Mirko. *Diseases in the Ancient Greek World*. Translated by M. Muellner. Baltimore: Johns Hopkins University Press, 1989.

Groce, Nora. *Everyone Here Spoke Sign Language: Hereditary Deafness on Martha's Vineyard*. Cambridge: Harvard University Press, 1985.

Grunwell, Pam. "Assessment of Articulation and Phonology." In *Assessment in Speech and Language Therapy*, edited by J. Beech and L. Harding, 49–67. London: Routledge, 1993.

Hagrup [Hirsch], Karen. "Culture and Disability: The Role of Oral History." *Oral History Review* 22 (1995): 1–27.

Hahn, Harlan. "Disability and Classical Aesthetic Canons." N.p., 1993.

Haller, Beth. "Rethinking Models of Media Representation of Disability." *Disability Studies Quarterly* 15, no. 2 (Spring 1995): 29–30.

Hands, Arthur Robinson. *Charities and Social Aid in Greece and Rome*. London: Thames and Hudson, 1968.

Hansen, Mogens Herman. *Demography and Democracy: The Number of Athenian Citizens in the Fourth Century B.C.* Denmark: Systime, 1985.

Hanson, Victor. *The Western Way of War: Infantry Battle in Classical Greece*. New York: Alfred Knopf, 1989.

Hardie, Margaret M. "The Evil Eye in Some Greek Villages of the Upper Haliakmon Valley in West Macedonia." In *The Evil Eye: A Folklore Casebook*, edited by A. Dundes, 107–23. Garland Folklore Casebooks, no. 2. New York: Garland Publishing, 1981.

Hare, Ronald. "The Antiquity of Diseases Caused by Bacteria and Viruses: A Review of the Problem from a Bacteriologist's Perspective." In *Diseases in Antiquity: A Survey of the Diseases, Injuries and Surgery of Early Populations*, edited by Don Brothwell and A. T. Sandison, 115–31. Springfield, Ill.: Charles C. Thomas, 1967.

Harris, William. *Ancient Literacy*. Cambridge: Harvard University Press, 1989.

————. "The Theoretical Possibility of Extensive Infanticide in the Graeco-Roman World." *Classical Quarterly* 32, no. 1 (1982): 114–16.

Hathway, Marion. *The Young Cripple and His Job*. Social Service Monograph, no. 4. Chicago: University of Chicago Press, 1928.

Helbing, Monica. "Der Altägyptische Augenkranke, sein Arzt und seine Götter." *Zuercher Medizingeschtiche* 141 (1980): 1–78.

Henderson, Jeffrey. *The Maculate Muse: Obscene Language in Attic Comedy*. 2d ed. New York: Oxford University Press, 1991.

Henry, Madeleine. *Prisoner of History: Aspasia of Miletus and Her Biographical Tradition*. New York: Oxford University Press, 1995.

Hubbard, Ruth. "Abortion and Disability: Who Should and Should Not Inhabit the World?" In *The Disability Studies Reader*, edited by Lennard Davis, 187–200. New York: Routledge, 1997.

Hull, John. *Touching the Rock: An Experience of Blindness*. New York: Pantheon, 1990.

Huys, Marc. "The Spartan Practice of Selective Infanticide and Its Parallels in Ancient Utopian Tradition." *Ancient Society* 27 (1996): 47–74.

Jackson, Ralph. "Roman Doctors and Their Instruments: Recent Research into Ancient Practice." *Journal of Roman Archaeology* 3 (1990): 5–27.

Janssens, Paul. *Paleopathology: Diseases and Injuries of Prehistoric Man.* Translated by Ida Dequeecker. London: John Baker, 1970.

Johnson, Robert E., and Carol Erting. "Ethnicity and Socialization in a Classroom for Deaf Children." In *The Sociolinguistics of the Deaf Community*, edited by C. Lucas, 41–83. New York: Academic Press, 1989.

Just, Roger. *Women in Athenian Law and Life.* New York: Routledge, 1989.

Karacoloff, Linda A., Carol Stube Hammersley, and Frederick J. Schneider. *Lower Extremity Amputation: A Guide to Functional Outcomes in Physical Therapy Management.* 2d ed. Gaithersburg, Md.: Aspen Publishing, 1992.

Kerr, Jean. "Assessment of Acquired Language Problems." In *Assessment in Speech and Language Therapy*, edited by J. Beech and L. Harding, 99–127. London: Routledge, 1993.

Killian, Hans. *Cold and Frost Injuries: Rewarming Damages: Biological, Angiological, and Clinical Aspects.* Disaster Medicine, no. 3. Berlin: Springer, 1981.

Koelbing, Huldrych. *Arzt und Patient in der antiken Welt.* Zurich: Artemis, 1977.

Kolk, Charles. *Assessment and Planning with the Visually Impaired.* Baltimore: University Park Press, 1981.

Kottek, Samuel. *Medicine and Hygiene in the Works of Flavius Josephus.* Studies in Ancient Medicine, no. 9. Leiden: E. J. Brill, 1994.

Kudlien, Fridolf. *Der Beginn des medizinischen Denkens bei den Griechen von Homer bis Hippocrates.* Zurich: Artemis, 1967.

———. *Die Sklaven in der Griechischen Medizin der Klassischen und Hellenistischen Zeit.* Forschungen zur Antiken Sklaverei. Band II. Weisbaden: Franz Steiner, 1968.

Kuhse, Helga, and Peter Singer. *Should the Baby Live? The Problem of Handicapped Infants.* New York: Oxford University Press, 1985.

Lacey, W. K. *The Family in Classical Greece.* Ithaca: Cornell University Press, 1968.

Lampropoulou, Venetta. "The History of Deaf Education in Greece." In *The Deaf Way: Perspectives from the International Conference on Deaf Culture*, edited by Carol Erting, R. C. Johnson, D. L. Smith, and B. D. Snider, 239–49. Washington, D.C.: Gallaudet University Press, 1995.

Landsman, Gail H. "Reconstructing Motherhood in the Age of 'Perfect' Babies: Mothers of Infants and Toddlers with Disabilities." *Signs* 24 (autumn 1998): 69–99.

Lane, Harlan. *When the Mind Hears: A History of the Deaf.* New York: Random House, 1985.

Lang, Mabel. *Cure and Cult in Ancient Corinth: A Guide to the Asklepion.* Princeton: American School of Classical Studies at Athens, 1977.

Langer, William L. "Infanticide: A Historical Survey." *History of Childhood Quarterly* 1, no. 3 (winter 1974): 353–65.

Lefkowitz, Mary. *The Lives of the Greek Poets.* Baltimore: Johns Hopkins University Press, 1981.

Leipoldt, Johannes. *Didymus der Blinde von Alexandria.* Texte und Untersuchungen zur Geschichte der Christlichen Literatur, no. 29.3. Leipzig: J. C. Hinrich, 1905.

Levi, Patricia E. "Principles and Mechanisms of Teratogenesis." In *Teratogens: Chemicals Which Cause Birth Defects*, 2d ed, edited by V. Kolb, 1–19. Amsterdam: Elsevier, 1993.

Linton, Simi. *Claiming Disability: Knowledge and Identity.* New York: New York University Press, 1998.

Longrigg, James. *Greek Rational Medicine: Philosophy and Medicine from Alcmaeon to the Alexandrians.* New York: Routledge, 1993.

Longmore, Paul. "Screening Stereotypes: Images of Disabled People." *Social Policy* 16, no. 1 (1985): 31–37.

Louck, Margaret. "Cultivating the Body: Anthropology and Epistemologies of Bodily Practice and Knowledge." *Annual Review of Anthropology* 22 (1993): 133–55.

Louis, P. "Monstres et monstruosités dans la Biologie d'Aristote." In *Le Monde Grec: Hommages à Claire Préaux,* edited by J. Bingen, G. Combier, and G. Nachtergal, 277–84. Brussels: Éditions de l'université de Bruxelles, 1978.

Lowenfeld, Berthold. *The Changing Status of the Blind: From Separation to Integration.* Springfield, Ill.: Charles C. Thomas, 1975.

Majno, Guido. *The Healing Hand: Man and Wound in the Ancient World.* Cambridge: Harvard University Press, 1975.

Makler, Paul Todd. "New Information on Nutrition in Ancient Greece." *Klio* 62 (1980): 317–19.

Manning, Lynn. "The Magic Wand." In *Staring Back: The Disability Experience from the Inside Out,* edited by K. Fries, 165. New York: Plume, 1997.

Manning, Walter. *Clinical Decision Making in the Diagnosis and Treatment of Fluency Disorders.* Albany: Delmar Publishers, 1996.

Mason, J. A., and K. R. Herrmann. "Universal Infant Hearing Screening by Automated Auditory Brainstem Response Measurement." *Pediatrics* 101 (1998): 221–28.

"Mass Media and Disability Links." Available at <http://saber.towson.edu~bhalle/disable.html>. Accessed November 21, 2002.

Masson O. "Le nom de Battos, fondateur de Cyrene." *Glotta* 54 (1976): 84–98.

Mateer, Catherine. "Neural Bases of Language." In *Neuropsychology of Stuttering,* edited by E. Bomberg, 1–38. Edmonton: University of Alberta Press, 1993.

Metzler, Karen. "If There's Life, Make It Worth Living." In *Infanticide and the Value of Life,* edited by Marvin Kohl, 172–79. Buffalo: Prometheus, 1978.

Michel, Clement J. "Osteoarthritis." *Primary Care* 20 (December 1993): 815–26.

Middleton, Donald B. "Infectious Arthritis." *Primary Care* 20 (December 1993): 943–53.

Minerva, Alganza Roldán. "La mujer en la historiografía griega helenística: Polibio, mujeres e historia viril." In *La mujer en el mundo mediterráneo antiguo,* edited by A. López, C. Martínez, and A. Pociña, 54–72. Granada: Universidad de Granada, 1990.

Mitchell, David. "The Frontier That Never Ends." *Ragged Edge* 1 (January/February 1997): 20–21.

Morens, David, and Robert Littman. "Epidemiology of the Plague of Athens."

Transactions and Proceedings of the American Philological Association 122 (1992): 271–304.

Ogden, Daniel. *The Crooked Kings of Ancient Greece.* London: Duckworth, 1997.

Oldenziel, Ruth. "The Historiography of Infanticide in Antiquity: A Literature Stillborn." In *Sexual Asymmetry: Studies in Ancient Society,* edited by Josine Blok and Peter Mason, 87–107. Amsterdam: J. C. Gieben, 1987.

O'Neill, Yves Violé. *Speech and Speech Disorders in Western Thought before 1600.* Westport, Conn.: Greenwood Press, 1980.

"Orthopedic Topics: Clubfoot." <http://www.orthoseek.com/articles /clubfoot.html>. Accessed 21 November 2002.

Ortner, Donald, and Walter G. J. Putschar. *Identification of Pathological Conditions in Human Skeletal Remains.* Smithsonian Contributions to Anthropology, no. 28. Washington, D.C.: Smithsonian Institution Press, 1985.

Patrick, Adam. "Disease in Antiquity: Greece and Rome." In *Diseases in Antiquity: A Survey of the Diseases, Injuries and Surgery of Early Populations,* edited by Don Brothwell and A. T. Sandison, 238–46. Springfield, Ill.: Charles C. Thomas, 1967.

Patterson, Cynthia. "'Not Worth the Rearing': The Causes of Infant Exposure in Ancient Greece." *Transactions of the American Philological Association* 115 (1985): 103–23.

Paulson, William. *Enlightenment, Romanticism, and the Blind in France.* Princeton: Princeton University Press, 1987.

Pennington, Jean. *Food Values of Portions Commonly Used.* 15th ed. New York: HarperCollins, 1989.

Pereira Da Cunha, M. C., and C. De Lemos. "Gesture in Hearing Mother–Deaf Child Interaction." In *From Gesture to Language in Hearing and Deaf Children,* edited by V. Volterra and Carol Erting, 178–86. New York: Springer, 1990.

Perez Estevez, Rosa Maria. *El Problema de los Vagos en la España del Siglo XVIII.* Madrid: Confederacion Española de Cajas Ahorros, 1976.

Pernick, Martin. *The Black Stork: Eugenics and the Death of "Defective" Babies in American Medicine and Motion Pictures since 1915.* New York: Oxford University Press, 1996.

Phillips, E. D. *Aspects of Greek Medicine.* Philadelphia: Charles Press, 1987.

Pinker, Steven. *The Language Instinct.* New York: William Morrow and Company, 1994.

Pomeroy, Sarah. "Infanticide in Hellenistic Greece." In *Images of Women in Antiquity,* edited by A. Cameron and A. Kuhrt, 207–22. 2d ed. Detroit: Wayne State University Press, 1993.

Porter, James, ed. *Constructions of the Classical Body.* Ann Arbor: University of Michigan Press, 1999.

Pötscher, W. "Der Stumme Sohn der Kroisos." *Zeitschrift für klinische Psychologie und Psychotherapie* 20 (1974): 367–68.

Pritchard, D. G. *Education and the Handicapped, 1760–1790.* London: Routledge, 1963.

Pryse-Phillips, William. "The Epidemiology of Multiple Sclerosis." In *Handbook of Multiple Sclerosis,* edited by S. Cook, 1–24. New York: Marcel Dekker, 1990.

Rabinowitz, Nancy Sorkin. "Female Speech and Female Sexuality: Euripides' *Hippolytus* as Model." *Helios* 13, no. 2 (1986): 127–40.

Ré, Juan Alejandro. *El Problema de la Mendicidad en Buenos Aires: Sus Causas y Remedios.* Buenos Aires: Talleres Gráficos Argentinos, 1938.

Reeder, Ellen D. "Women and Men in Classical Greece." In *Pandora: Women in Classical Greece,* edited by Ellen D. Reeder, 20–31. Baltimore: Trustees of the Walters Art Gallery and Princeton University Press, 1995.

Reiber, R. W., and Jeffrey Wollock. "The Historical Roots of the Theory and Therapy of Stuttering." In *The Problem of Stuttering: Theory and Therapy,* edited by R. W. Reiber, 3–24. New York: Elsevier, 1977.

Reinhold, Meyer. "The Generation Gap in Antiquity." In *The Conflict of Generations in Ancient Greece and Rome,* edited by S. Bertman, 15–54. Amsterdam: Grüner, 1976.

Renger, Johannes. "Kranke, Krüppel, Debile: Eine Randgruppe in Alten Orient?" In *Außenseiter und Randgruppen: Beiträge zu einer Sozialgeschichte des Alten Orients,* edited by Volkert Haas, 113–24. Konstanz: Univ. Verlag Konstanz, 1992.

Retsas, Spyros. "On the Antiquity of Cancer: From Hippocrates to Galen." In *Paleo-oncology: The Antiquity of Cancer,* edited by Spyros Retsas, 41–58. London: Farrand, 1986.

Rhodes, P. J. *A Commentary on the Aristotelian* Athenaion Politeia. Oxford: Clarendon Press, 1981.

Richter, Gisela M. A. "Grotesques and the Mime." *American Journal of Archaeology* 17 (1913): 151–52.

Rose [Edwards], Martha L. "Deaf and Dumb in Ancient Greece." In *The Disability Studies Reader,* edited by Lennard Davis, 29–51. New York: Routledge, 1997.

———. Review of *The Eye of the Beholder: Deformity and Disability in the Graeco-Roman World,* by Robert Garland. *Disability Studies Quarterly* 16 (spring 1996): 36–37.

———. "'Let There Be a Law That No Deformed Child Shall Be Reared': The Cultural Context of Deformity in the Ancient Greek World." *Ancient History Bulletin* 10 (July 1997): 79–92.

———. "Women and Physical Disability in Ancient Greece." *Ancient World* 29, no. 1 (1998): 3–9.

Rosner, Edwin. "Terminologische Hinweise auf die Herkunft der frühen griechischen Medizin." In *Medizingeschichte in unserer Zeit,* edited by H. Eulner, G. Mann, G. Preiser, R. Winau, and O. Winkelmann, 1–22. Stuttgart: Ferdinand Enke, 1971.

Roush, Jackson. "Screening for Hearing Loss and Otitis Media: Basic Principles." In *Screening for Hearing Loss and Otitis Media in Children,* edited by Jackson Roush, 3–32. San Diego: Singular, 2001.

Rousselle, Aline. *Porneia: On Desire and the Body in Antiquity: Family, Sexuality and Social Relations in Past Times.* Translated by F. Pheasant. New York: Oxford University Press, 1988.

Ruschenbusch, Eberhard. "Tribut und Bürgerzahl im Ersten Athenischen Seebund." *Zeitschrift für Papyrologie und Epigraphik* 53 (1983): 125–48.

Rustin, Lena, and Armin Kuhr. *Social Skills and the Speech Impaired*. London: Taylor and Francis, 1989.

Salazar, Christine F. *The Treatment of War Wounds in Graeco-Roman Antiquity*. Studies in Ancient Medicine, no. 21. Leiden: E. J. Brill, 2000.

Sallares, Robert. *The Ecology of the Ancient Greek World*. Ithaca: Cornell University Press, 1991.

Salomon, Gerhard. "Hearing Problems and the Elderly." *Danish Medical Bulletin Special Supplement Series on Gerontology* 33 (suppl. 3; 1986): 1–17.

Samson, S. Y. "Historical Views of 'Normalcy.'" *Collegium Antropologicum* 16 (1992): 251–56.

Schaps, David. *Economic Rights of Women in Ancient Greece*. Edinburgh: Edinburgh University Press, 1979.

———. "The Women of Greece in Wartime." *Classical Philology* 77 (1982): 193–212.

Scheetz, Nanci. *Orientation to Deafness*. Boston: Allyn and Bacon, 1993.

Scheidel, Walter. "The Most Silent Women of Greece and Rome: Rural Labor and Women's Life in the Ancient World." Part 1. *Greece and Rome* 42, no. 2 (October 1995): 202–17.

———. "The Most Silent Women of Greece and Rome: Rural Labor and Women's Life in the Ancient World." Part 2. *Greece and Rome* 43, no. 1 (April 1996): 1–10.

Scrimshaw, Susan C. M. "Infanticide in Human Populations: Societal and Individual Concerns." In *Infanticide: Comparative and Evolutionary Perspectives*, edited by Glenn Haufater and Sarah Blaffer Hrdy, 439–62. New York: Aldine Publishing Company, 1984.

Sealey, Raphael. *Demosthenes and His Time: A Study in Defeat*. New York: Oxford University Press, 1993.

———. *Women and Law in Classical Greece*. Chapel Hill: University of North Carolina Press, 1990.

Seeberg, Axel. "Hephaistos Rides Again." *Journal of Hellenic Studies* 85 (1965): 102–9.

Segal, Charles. *Art, Gender, and Communication in* Alcestis, Hippolytus, *and* Hecuba. Durham: Duke University Press, 1993.

Seringe, R., P. Herlin, R. Kohler, D. Moulies, A. Tanguy, and A. Zouari. "A New Articulated Splint for Clubfeet." In *The Clubfoot: The Present and a View of the Future*, edited by George Simons, 187–90. New York: Springer, 1994.

Shapiro, Joseph P. *No Pity: People with Disabilities Forging a New Civil Rights Movement*. New York: Random House, 1993.

Sheehan, Joseph G. *Stuttering: Research and Therapy*. New York: Harper and Row, 1970.

Silverman, Franklin. *Communication for the Speechless*. Boston: Allyn and Bacon, 1995.

———. *Stuttering and Other Fluency Disorders*. 2d ed. Boston: Allyn and Bacon, 1996.

Simons, George. "Etiological Theories of CTEV." In *The Clubfoot: The Present and a View of the Future*, edited by George Simons, 2. New York: Springer, 1994.

Sines, George, and Yannis A. Sakellarakis. "Lenses in Antiquity." *American Journal of Archaeology* 91 (1987): 191–96.

Sommer, Alfred. *Nutritional Blindness: Xerophthalmia and Keratomalacia.* New York: Oxford University Press, 1982.

Sommers, Ronald. *Articulation Disorders.* Englewood Cliffs, N.J.: Prentice-Hall, 1983.

Souques, A. *Étapes de la neurologie dans l'antiquité grecque.* Paris: Libraries de L'Académie de Médicine, 1936.

von Staden, Heinrich. *Herophilus: The Art of Medicine in Early Alexandria.* Cambridge: Cambridge University Press, 1989.

———. "Incurability and Hopelessness: The *Hippocratic Corpus.*" In *La maladie et les maladies dans la Collection hippocratique: Actes du VIe Colloque International Hippocratique,* edited by P. Potter, G. Maloney, and J. Desautels, 75–112. City of Québec: Les Éditions du Sphinx, 1990.

Starkweather, C. Woodruff, and Janet Givens-Ackerman. *Stuttering.* Austin: Pro-Ed, 1997.

Starr, Chester. *The Economic and Social Growth of Early Greece, 800–500 B.C.* New York: Oxford University Press, 1977.

Starz, Terence W., and Edward B. Miller. "Diagnosis and Treatment of Rheumatoid Arthritis." *Primary Care* 20 (December 1993): 827–37.

Stead, William, and Asim K. Dutt. "Epidemiology and Host Factors." In *Tuberculosis,* edited by D. Schlossberg, 1–15. 3d ed. New York: Springer, 1994.

Stengel, Paul. *Die Griechischen Kultusaltertümer.* Munich: C. H. Beck, 1920.

Stiker, Henri-Jacques. *Corps infirmes et sociétés.* Paris: Aubier Montage, 1982.

Stockton, David. *The Classical Athenian Democracy.* Oxford: Oxford University Press, 1990.

Stokoe, William. "Language, Prelanguage, and Sign Language." *Seminars in Speech and Language* 11 (1990): 92–99.

———. "Seeing Clearly through Fuzzy Speech." *Sign Language Studies* 82 (spring 1994): 85–91.

"Stottervereniging Demosthenes." Available at <http://www.stotteren.nl/demosthenes>. Accessed November 2000.

Temkin, Oswei. *The Falling Sickness: A History of Epilepsy from the Greeks to the Beginnings of Modern Neurology.* Baltimore: Johns Hopkins University Press, 1971.

Thalmann, W. G. "Thersites: Comedy, Scapegoats, and Heroic Ideology in the *Iliad.*" *Transactions and Proceedings of the American Philological Association* 118 (1988): 1.

Thomas, Rosiland. *Literacy and Orality in Ancient Greece.* Cambridge: Cambridge University Press, 1992.

Thomson, Rosemarie Garland. *Extraordinary Bodies: Figuring Physical Disability in American Culture and Literature.* New York: Columbia University Press, 1997.

Tobin, Michael J. "Blindness in Later Life: Myths, Attitudes and Reality." *British Journal of Visual Impairment* 13, no. 2 (1995): 69–75.

Trilling, Diana. "Reading by Ear." *Civilization* 1 (November/December 1994): 54–57.

van Hook, La Rue. "The Exposure of Infants at Athens." *Transactions and Proceedings of the American Philological Association* 41 (1920): 134–45.

van Riper, Charles. *The Nature of Stuttering.* 2d ed. Englewood Cliffs, N.J.: Prentice-Hall, 1982.

van Straten, F. T. "Gifts for the Gods." In *Faith, Hope and Worship,* edited by H. S. Versnel, 65–151. Leiden: E. J. Brill, 1981.

van N. Viljoen, G. "Plato and Aristotle on the Exposure of Infants at Athens." *Acta Classica* 2 (1959): 58–69.

Vaughan, C. Edwin. *Social and Cultural Perspectives on Blindness: Barriers to Community Integration.* Springfield, Ill.: Charles C. Thomas, 1998.

Versnel, H. S. "Religious Mentality in Ancient Prayer." In *Faith, Hope and Worship,* edited by H. S. Versnel, 1–64. Leiden: E. J. Brill, 1981.

Vlahogiannis, Nicholas. Review of *Dwarfs in Ancient Egypt and Greece,* by Veronique Dasen. *Medical History* 39 (1995): 119–20.

Wade, Cheryl Marie. "I am Not One of The." In *The Disability Studies Reader,* edited by Lennard Davis, 408. New York: Routledge, 1997.

Walcot, Peter. *Greek Peasants, Ancient and Modern: A Comparison of Social and Moral Values.* New York: Barnes and Noble, 1970.

Warkany, Josef. "Congenital Malformations in the Past." *Journal of Chronic Disease* 10 (1959): 84–96.

Weiler, Ingomar. "Soziale Randgruppen in der antiken Welt: Einführung und wissenschaftsgeschichtliche Aspekte: Ausgewählte Literatur zur historichen Randgruppenforschung." In *Soziale Randgruppen und Außenseiter im Alterum,* edited by Ingomar Weiler, 11–24. Graz: Leykam, 1988.

Weir, Robert F. *Selective Nontreatment of Handicapped Newborns: Moral Dilemmas in Neonatal Medicine.* New York: Oxford University Press, 1984.

Wells, Calvin. *Bones, Bodies and Disease: Evidence of Disease and Abnormality in Early Man.* Ancient Peoples and Places, no. 37. Bristol: Western Printing Services, 1964.

"Where Helen and Alexander Stopped." Available at <http://www.wsu.edu:8080/~dee/GREECE/SPARTA.HTM>. Accessed July 1999.

Wiles, David. *Greek Theatre Performance: An Introduction.* Cambridge: Cambridge University Press, 2000.

Williams, Donna. *Somebody Somewhere: Breaking Free from the World of Autism.* New York: Times Books, 1994.

Williams, Pat. "Christopher Reeve: What's It Gonna Take?" *Ragged Edge* 1 (January/February 1997): 16–19.

Winckelmann, Johann Joachim. "On the Imitation of the Painting and Sculpture of the Greeks." 1755. In *Winckelmann: Writings on Art,* edited by David Irwin. London: Phaidon, 1972.

Winter, Thomas. "Lippus, Lippire, Lippitudo." Paper presented at the annual meeting of the American Philological Association, San Diego, Calif., 29 December, 1995.

Wolf, George. "A Historical Note on the Mode of Administration of Vitamin A for the Cure of Night Blindness." *The American Journal of Clinical Nutrition* 31 (February 1978): 290–92.

Wolfe, Kathi. "Don't Bug Me!" *Mainstream* 20 (April 1996): 23–25.

———. "The Write Stuff." *Mainstream* 21 (October 1996): 32–34.

Worman, Nancy. "The Ethics of Style in Sophocles' *Philoctetes.*" Paper presented at the annual meeting of the American Philological Association, Atlanta, Ga., 30 December 1994.

Wright, Jannet. "Assessment of Children with Special Needs." In *Assessment in Speech and Language Therapy,* edited by J. Beech and L. Harding, 128–48. New York: Routledge, 1993.

Wu, Yeongchi, and Preston Flanigan. "Rehabilitation of the Lower Extremity Amputee." In *Gangrene and Severe Ischemia of the Lower Extremities,* edited by J. Bergan and J. T. Yao, 435–53. New York: Grune and Stratton, 1978.

Wylie, Graham. "Demosthenes the General: Protagonist in a Greek Tragedy?" *Greece and Rome* 40, no. 1 (April 1993): 20–30.

Young, Richard. *Age-Related Cataract.* New York: Oxford University Press, 1991.

Zimbler, S. "Nonoperative Management of the Equinovarus Foot: Long-Term Results." In *The Clubfoot: The Present and a View of the Future,* edited by George Simons, 191–95. New York: Springer, 1994.

Živanović, Srboljub. *Ancient Diseases: The Elements of Paleopathology.* Translated by L. Edwards. New York: Pica Press, 1982.

Index

This is not an Index Locorum; names of ancient authors are listed only when they are mentioned within the narration.

Pericles, 61, 62

Philip II, 4, 44

Philoctetes. *See under* Literary and mythological figures

Physicians. *See* Doctors

Pity, 6, 48, 66, 90, 93, 97, 99

Plague, 22, 86. *See also* Disease; Epidemic disease; Infection

Plato, 13, 20, 30, 31, 32, 33, 34, 38, 42, 47, 58, 59, 62, 75, 76, 81, 90

Pliny, 14, 24, 26, 85

Plutarch, 13, 16, 20, 26, 27, 31, 32–33, 34, 38, 44, 53, 55, 56, 57, 59, 60, 63, 66, 68, 77, 81, 82, 84, 91, 92

Poetry (modern), x, 5, 93

Polybius, 92

Prelingual deafness, 72, 74, 99

Prenatal screening. *See* Amniocentesis testing

Priests, 42, 43, 60. *See also* Assumptions about disability, religious

Prophecy; prophets. *See* Seers

Prosthetics, 26–27, 65. *See also* Amputation

Prostitutes, 61, 62

Psychiatric disability. *See* Mental illness

Pythia, 60. *See also* Delphic oracle

Quadriplegia, 3, 14, 65

Quintilian, 57

Religion. *See* Assumptions about disability, religious; Priests

Religious assumptions about disability. *See* Assumptions about disability, religious

Renaissance imagery, 7, 10

Ridicule. *See* Mockery of disabled

Scapegoating; scapegoats, 43. *See also* Assumptions about disability, religious

School of Athens (Raphael), 9

Seers, 79, 80

Sight impairment, 27, 46, 79–94. *See also* Blind

Sign language, 74–75, 76. *See also* Gesture

Skeletal material/remains, 5, 21, 26, 38, 51

Slavery; slaves, 40, 54, 72, 75, 91

Social construction. *See* Cultural/social construction

Society for Disability Studies, 3, 6

Socrates, 9, 13, 75, 76

Sophocles, 19, 39, 58, 80, 88

Soranus, 32, 33–34, 35

Spartan infanticide, 2, 29, 30, 32–33, 34, 49

Speech impairments, 11, 50–65. *See also* Lisp; Stutter

Spina bifida, 23, 31, 52

Staffs, 26, 44, 88. *See also* Canes; Crutches

State aid. *See* Pension

Statuary, 11, 36, 37

Sterility, 47. *See also* Women

Strabo, 55, 68

Stroke. *See* Cardiovascular accident (CVA)/disease

Stutter; stuttering, 7, 51, 52, 54, 55, 57, 65

Supercrip, 2, 99

Swaddling, 23, 38

Teiresias. *See under* Literary and mythological figures

Telethon, 99

Teratology, 7. *See also* Monstrosity

Thamyris. *See under* Literary and mythological figures

Theophrastus, 12

Thersites. *See under* Literary and mythological figures

Thucydides, 22, 86

Tragedy, 19, 24, 60, 79. *See also* Aeschylus; Euripides; Sophocles

Tuberculosis, 14, 22

Ugliness, 12, 13, 36, 37, 43. *See also* Beauty

Utopia, 3, 32, 34, 37, 49, 66

Printed and bound by CPI Group (UK) Ltd, Croydon, CR0 4YY

09/06/2025

14685646-0005